The Living
Chess Game

THE LIVING CHESS GAME

Fine Arts Activities for Kids 9–14

Alexey W. Root

LIBRARIES UNLIMITED

AN IMPRINT OF ABC-CLIO, LLC
Santa Barbara, California • Denver, Colorado • Oxford, England

Library of Congress Cataloging-in-Publication Data

Root, Alexey W.
    The living chess game : fine arts activities for kids 9–14 / Alexey W. Root.
      p. cm.
    Includes bibliographical references and index.
    ISBN 978-1-59884-380-4 (alk. paper) — ISBN 978-1-59884-381-1 (ebook)
1. Living chess.   I. Title.
    GV1318.R66   2011
    794.1'7—dc22   2010041571

ISBN: 978-1-59884-380-4
EISBN: 978-1-59884-381-1

15 14 13 12 11   1 2 3 4 5

This book is also available on the World Wide Web as an eBook.
Visit www.abc-clio.com for details.

Libraries Unlimited
An Imprint of ABC-CLIO, LLC

ABC-CLIO, LLC
130 Cremona Drive, P.O. Box 1911
Santa Barbara, California 93116-1911

This book is printed on acid-free paper ∞

Manufactured in the United States of America

For librarians
Jody Braswell (Ector County Independent School District) and
WyLaina Hildreth (Denton Public Library)

CONTENTS

Chapter 1

FINE ARTS AND CHESS

Activities Fit Available Time

The Living Chess Game: Fine Arts Activities for Kids 9–14 provides librarians, core subject teachers, fine arts directors, chess coaches, parents, volunteers, and after-school instructors with 11 activities that culminate in a living chess game performance. Living chess games, where humans act as the **chessmen**, are staged at libraries, schools, festivals, parks, and Renaissance Fairs. *The Living Chess Game* prepares readers to join this 1,300-year-old tradition. Chess terms are in boldface when first used and are defined in the glossary.

Within the 11 activities, children compose music, choreograph movements, research chess, design scenery, write a script, and act. If you have more than 12 hours of instructional time and work with children ages 9–14, teach each activity in the order presented. If you work with younger children, or if you have limited instructional time, shorten or skip some of the activities. For example, you might create the music, choreography, set, and script. Or if you are not comfortable teaching music, skip chapter 2 and have a nonmusical living chess game. Children can still be the living chess game's actors. If you teach children infrequently or if children attend irregularly, then organize a talent show (see *Activity Twelve*) instead of a living chess game.

Whether taught as written or modified, *The Living Chess Game: Fine Arts Activities for Kids 9–14* brings music, dance, visual arts, theater, and chess to children. Fine arts training, guest artists, musical instruments, or a dedicated performance venue are not required. As Gelineau (2004, p. 17) wrote, "A teacher need not be an artist, musician, dancer, or other arts professional in order to provide a nurturing arts climate that will vitalize the learning process." If available, however, fine arts resources may be incorporated. Gelineau (2004, p. 14) suggested, "First, believe you can, and then call upon available specialists as well as parents and other community resources for additional ideas. Many are delighted to be asked and talents abound."

The Living Chess Game: Fine Arts Activities for Kids 9–14 provides enough chess information for children to perform, with understanding, as living chessmen. Living chess games may have predetermined **moves** (a script) or be a live contest between two players. I recommend scripted games. From Appendix C, choose a script (a famous game or **problem**) based on the number of chessmen (actors) available. Fewer than 32 actors are required with a script, for three reasons. First, the script may begin at a **position** from a **middlegame** or an **endgame,** after **trades** or **sacrifices** have occurred. Therefore, fewer chessmen are on the board for the start of the script. Second, since it is known in advance which chessmen will move, set decorations may represent stationary chessmen. Third, a chessman captured early may double as a chessman moving later in the game. As noted in the essay "Putting on a Play: Step-by-Step" (ArtsAlive.ca, 2009):

> Be realistic when casting your production. It's rare that a play has the same number of actors as there are roles. This means that actors often play more than one role. Doubling, as it is called, is a challenge and can be great fun! ("The script," para. 2)

In contrast, an unscripted game begins with 32 chessmen in their starting positions. Since it is not known which chessmen will move, all must be portrayed by actors. Yet some of the 32 actors may stand on their original squares for the entire game. For those stationary actors, the living chess game might seem very dull.

Fine Arts Standards

The activities address content standards from the National Standards for Arts Education (Music Educators National Conference [MENC], 1994). Teaching fine arts stimulates children's creativity and exposes them to important aspects of human culture. Fine arts instruction also helps with academics, according to advocates of Howard Gardner's theory of multiple intelligences. As Gelineau (2004) wrote:

> Assuming that all education should include the arts as cognitive domains or forms of understanding, advocates of Gardner's theories maintain that there is power in education *through* the arts as well. The argument is that if a student cannot comprehend traditional academic subjects verbally or

Table showing the connection of activities in *The Living Chess Game* to the National Standards for Arts Education (MENC, 1994).

Activity	National Standard for Arts Education addressed by Activity
One: The Music of the Knight	Music, Content Standard 4: Composing and arranging music within specified guidelines.
Two: From Moves to Grooves	Music, Content Standard 3: Improvising melodies, variations, and accompaniments.
Three: Chess in Concert	Music, Content Standard 5: Reading and notating music.
Four: Chess Boxing	Dance, Content Standard 1: Identifying and demonstrating movement elements and skills in performing dance.
Five: Brains and Brawn	Dance, Content Standard 6: Making connections between dance and other disciplines.
Six: The Art of Chess	Visual Arts, Content Standard 5: Reflecting upon and assessing the characteristics and merits of their work and the work of others.
Seven: All the World's a Chessboard	Visual Arts, Content Standard 2: Using knowledge of structures and functions.
Eight: Immortal and Evergreen	Theater, Content Standard 1: Script writing by the creation of improvisations and scripted scenes based on personal experience and heritage, imagination, literature, and history.
Nine: No Small Parts	Theater, Content Standard 2: Acting by assuming roles and interacting in improvisations.
Ten: Tech and Check	Theater, Content Standard 3: Designing by developing environments for improvised and scripted scenes.
Eleven: The Living Chess Game	Theater, Content Standard 4: Directing by organizing rehearsals for improvised and scripted scenes.
Twelve: Talent Show	Theater, Content Standard 6: Comparing and incorporating art forms by analyzing methods of presentation and audience response for theatre, dramatic media (such as film, television, and electronic media), and other art forms.

Figure 1.1.
National standards addressed by activities.

From *The Living Chess Game: Fine Arts Activities for Kids 9–14* by Alexey W. Root. Santa Barbara, CA: Libraries Unlimited. Copyright © 2011.

linguistically, that student can understand them visually, musically, or even kinesthetically. (p. 13, italics in original)

The Living Chess Game activities are cross-curricular with academic subjects. For example, designing a **board** (visual arts) involves measurement (math).

Overview of Chapters

Chapter 1: Fine Arts and Chess explains the purpose of *The Living Chess Game.* I tell where I field-tested the activities in chapters 2–4. The last section of chapter 1 recommends chess equipment. At the end of the chapter is Figure 1.5, a chart of the chess knowledge needed for each activity.

Chapters 2, 3, and 4 contain fine arts activities. Each activity has the following sections: content standard, objectives, resources and materials, procedure, and assessment. Some activities include reproducibles. Besides listing the optional resources and needed materials, the "resources and materials" section serves two additional purposes. First, it explains the cultural reference in each activity's title. Second, when applicable, it lists opportunities for parental involvement such as tech support and attending children's performances. The first seven activities take 40 minutes each. Activities eight through eleven—script writing, auditions, costuming, rehearsal, and performance of the living chess game—require additional time. *Activity Twelve: Talent Show* is independent from this book's other activities and requires minimal instructional time.

Chapter 2: Music has three activities. In *Activity One: The Music of the Knight,* children write two lines about their favorite chessman: **knight, queen, rook, bishop, king,** or **pawn.** The lines give the chessman's name and tell how it moves. In *Activity Two: From Moves to Grooves,* children determine the time signature and note values for their *Activity One* lyrics. Children chant their compositions while moving like a chessman. For *Activity Three: Chess in Concert,* children sing a C major melody to accompany their rhythmic lyrics from prior activities. They record their compositions using music notation.

Chapter 3: Dance and Visual Arts has two dance and two visual arts activities. In *Activity Four: Chess Boxing* children choreograph **captures** by their favorite chessman. For *Activity Five: Brains and Brawn* children practice physical and mental warm-ups, to be used before dancing or playing chess. For *Activity Six: The Art of Chess* children appreciate chess **sets** and boards as visual art. For *Activity Seven: All the World's a Chessboard* children borrow design ideas from the admired chess sets and boards in *Activity Six.*

Chapter 4: Theater has five activities. The first four activities prepare for a living chess game performance. In *Activity Eight: Immortal and Evergreen* children write a script. First, they study a famous chess game or problem corresponding to the number of actors in their class. The script incorporates prior work from *Activity Three* (musical themes for the moves of chessmen) and *Activity Four* (choreography to represent the chessmen's captures). In *Activity Nine: No Small Parts* children audition by performing excerpts from *Activity Eight*'s script. Most children will be cast as living chessmen. One or two actors will provide **annotations** (narration) to the living chess game. For *Activity Ten: Tech and Check* children, staff, and parent volunteers collaboratively create scenery, costumes, and makeup based on designs from *Activity Seven*. For *Activity Eleven: The Living Chess Game* children first use warm-ups from *Activity Five* or other warm-ups that you have chosen for them. For the first rehearsal, children sit in a circle and read through the script together. For subsequent rehearsals, children rehearse the living chess game. After rehearsals are completed, the children perform for an audience. An alternative for exploring the fine arts, and separate from the living chess game activities, is a talent show. *Activity Twelve: Talent Show* allows children to rehearse, perform, and evaluate fine arts performances.

Chapter 5: Chess Basics contains the rules of chess, **algebraic notation**, and Internet sites for practicing chess. Appendix A: Answer Key includes samples of children's work from my teaching of the 12 activities in chapters 2–4. In Appendix B: References I list references and provide a description of each. I also list photo credits. Appendix C: Chess Scripts has chess problems and famous games appropriate for living chess games of different sizes (from 3 to 34 actors). The glossary defines the chess terms used in the book.

Kid-Tested Activities

I first tested the activities in this book at the MOSAIC (Marvelous Opportunities Scheduled as Individual Courses) summer enrichment courses, August 3–7, 2009. My students ranged in age from 8 to 13, plus one adult (the mother of one of the eight-year-olds). My 9–10:30 A.M. class had 11 students, and my 10:30 A.M. to noon class had 13 students. The parent information letter is in Appendix A. In both classes, I taught *Activities One, Four, Six, Seven, Eight,* and *Eleven. Activity Ten* was completed outside of class time: Students brought in costumes and props from home. The MOSAIC director, Tracy Fisher, created our chessboard stage, pictured in chapter 4 (Figure 4.5). In addition to participating in the fine arts activities, students played **ladder** games with each other and an end-of-week **simul** against me.

I also taught a Living Chess Game class at the North Branch of the Denton Public Library. The library class met weekly at 2:30–3:15 P.M. from September 3 to November 19 and had a performance at 4 P.M. on November 24, 2009. The class time conflicted with public school hours, but it attracted homeschooling families. The performance time, however, allowed public school students to attend. Nearby Evers Park Elementary dismissed at 3 P.M., and next-door Strickland Middle School dismissed at 3:35 P.M.

A press release and the Denton Public Library (North Branch) calendar, reproduced in Appendix A, publicized the classes and performance. A cast member's parent captured our November 24th performance on video. To view the nine-minute video, search YouTube for "Denton Living Chess" or try this URL: http://www.youtube.com/watch?v=yDW1LVS5n8k.

Since there were 12 weeks of classes before the performance, I taught the first 11 activities in this book. By popular demand of the children, the Simon Says game was repeated almost every week. Bronson and Merryman (2009, p. 168) wrote, "The simple game of Simon Says, for instance, entices a child to copy the leader yet requires the kid to pay close attention and exercise intermittent restraint." Simon Says assessed children's knowledge of chessmen's movement, as the room we used had a carpeted floor with multicolored squares. Each carpet square served as a chess square for a child (living chessman). I was the leader at each game's start. I also used Simon Says to burn up extra energy. For example, sometimes Simon said to jump up and down. As the game progressed, eliminated children took turns being the leader. Thus Simon Says also helped us practice listening to each other.

Though each fine arts activity took 40 minutes, we could keep the library meeting room for 1.5 hours. Therefore, I brought chess sets, boards, and a **demonstration board**. I often taught chess. For example, during *Activity Two*'s week, I taught king and two rooks versus king (Root, 2006, pp. 64–65, 99). During *Activity Four*'s week, I taught chess mazes (Root, 2008, pp. 58–59). Alongside *Activity Five* I taught the Scholar's Mate (Root, 2009, pp. 39–41). After completing that week's fine arts activity, paired children practiced the chess drill I'd showed them and then played chess for fun. For weeks when I did not offer new chess instruction, children played chess for fun immediately after the fine arts activity. Many children stayed for 1–1.5 hours. Most homeschooling parents stayed also, but others dropped off their children. Attendance ranged from 5 children (for the first class) to 11 (for *Activity Five*). Over the 12 weeks, the mode attendance was 6 children. The age range was 7–14 years old.

For the spring semester of 2010, I volunteered teaching chess in the Communities in Schools North Texas (CISNT) after-school program at Strickland Middle School. My chess club met from 3:40 to 5:00 P.M. Tuesday afternoons from January through May. During the snack time of our fourth meeting, I noticed one child model-walking, one child dancing, and another child singing. Another child showed me his artwork on his drawing pad. Back in the classroom were two children's violins. After my snack time observations, I decided to have a talent show. I approached the CISNT site coordinator, Michele Bentley, with my idea. The talent show would not be just for the children in chess club but for the roughly 80 children who attended CISNT at Strickland. Some children attended just a few days a week or for only part of the after-school program each day. But many children were there Monday through Friday and were not picked up until

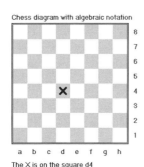

Figure 1.2.
Demonstration board.

the program's daily 5:45 P.M. end time. After some e-mails, a planning meeting, and the beginning of rehearsals, Michele and I set our audition date (March 23, 3:40–5 P.M.) and our talent show date (March 30, 5–5:45 P.M., so that some parents could attend). More about the talent show is in *Activity Twelve.*

I submitted this book's manuscript to my editor, Sharon Coatney, in April of 2010. She suggested revising Chapter 2: Music. I kept the same three activities, but I improved their clarity and added worksheets. I tested those revised activities from June 7 to 11, 2010, at MOSAIC. Enrolled in my chess courses were 10 children (9–10:30 class time) and 8 children and 1 parent (10:30 to noon class time). All the children were rising fourth through eighth graders, except for a six-year-old attending with his mother.

Chess Equipment and Knowledge

Several of the activities require that the instructor demonstrate chess moves in a whole class instructional setting. If you are teaching more than 10 children at once, buy a demonstration board. The cost for a 36-inch-square demonstration board with **pieces** and pawns, shown in Figure 1.2, is around $30 (including shipping) from American Chess Equipment (http://www.amchesseq.com). I also shop American Chess Equipment for my other chess supplies. There are other good Internet and brick-and-mortar retailers for chess equipment. Or ask the **United States Chess Federation (USCF)** for equipment sales and retailer recommendations.

If you teach fewer than 10 children, you may have them crowd around a regular-sized chess set and board rather than a demonstration board. For a couple of the activities and for children to play chess, acquire one chess set and board for every two children. Best are boards with algebraic notation marked around the outside borders. In algebraic notation, **files** are labeled a–h, and **ranks** are labeled 1–8. As shown in the **diagram** in Figure 1.3, a square is described file-first, followed by rank. Figure 1.3 shows a square on the d-file and fourth rank. Boards with notation are often sold with a **Staunton** set. To meet **tournament** and teaching standards, yet keep costs low, match a solid-plastic set (with a king 3.75 inches high) with a 20-inch vinyl board. If ordered in quantity, the cost for each board-and-set combination works out to about $6. In Figure 1.4, a

Figure 1.3.
Algebraic square naming.

Figure 1.4.
Children using standard chess
equipment.

10-year-old boy and a 9-year-old girl play chess on such a set and board. As mentioned in *Science, Math, Checkmate* (Root, 2008, pp. 6–7), free boards and sets are available for qualified schools from the U.S. Chess Trust (http://www.uschesstrust.com/). **Clocks** are useful if the children will be playing in tournaments.

Figure 1.5 is a chart of what chess knowledge is required for each activity.

Table showing the chess knowledge required by the activities in *The Living Chess Game.* Chapter 5 and the activities teach the required chess knowledge.

Activity or Activities	Chess Knowledge
One: The Music of the Knight; Two: From Moves to Grooves; Three: Chess in Concert	How the pieces and pawns move.
Four: Chess Boxing	How the pieces and pawns capture.
Five: Brains and Brawn	How to play a chess game. A "Pawn Game" (Root, 2008, pp. 16–19) may be substituted, if children are not yet confident with the pieces.
Six: The Art of Chess	Recognizing the chessmen.
Seven: All the World's a Chessboard	Place a board so that a white square is in the right hand corner. Dark squares and light squares alternate within eight files (labeled a–h) and eight ranks (labeled 1–8).
Eight: Immortal and Evergreen	How to read algebraic chess notation and all rules of chess.
Nine: No Small Parts	Recognizing the chessmen and knowing their moves and captures. Algebraic notation knowledge helpful.
Ten: Tech and Check	No chess knowledge required
Eleven: The Living Chess Game	Knowing how the chessman one is portraying moves and captures. Algebraic notation knowledge helpful.
Twelve: Talent Show	No chess knowledge required.

Figure 1.5.
Chess knowledge required by activities.

From *The Living Chess Game: Fine Arts Activities for Kids 9–14* by Alexey W. Root. Santa Barbara, CA: Libraries Unlimited. Copyright © 2011.

Chapter 2

MUSIC

This chapter has three activities. In *Activity One: The Music of the Knight,* children write two lines about their favorite chessman: knight, queen, rook, bishop, king, or pawn. The lines give the chessman's name and tell how it moves. In *Activity Two: From Moves to Grooves,* children determine the time signature and note values for their *Activity One* lyrics. Children chant their compositions while moving like a chessman. For *Activity Three: Chess in Concert,* children sing a C major melody to accompany their rhythmic lyrics from prior activities. They record their compositions using music notation.

Activity One: The Music of the Knight

Content standard. Music, Content Standard 4: Composing and arranging music within specified guidelines.

Objectives. Children learn, or review, how the chessmen move. Children compose lyrics that name a chessman and describe its movements. Children create chess diagrams that show a chessman's movements.

Resources and materials. Demonstration board; one chess set and board. Each child should have a pencil or pen and Figure 2.1. If including the optional Simon Says game, a large room or outdoor area is necessary.

The activity title *The Music of the Knight* refers to a similarly named song from the musical *The Phantom of the Opera.* A study guide for *The Phantom of the Opera,* with discussion questions and information about

To make a chess diagram, use the following abbreviations: K for king, Q for queen, R for rook, B for bishop, N for knight, and P for pawn. Circle the chessman's abbreviation if you want to show a black chessman. For example, R is a white rook but ® is a black rook. The first two diagrams below show a white king's moves (on the left diagram) and a black king's moves (on the right diagram). Under the diagrams are two lines of lyrics naming the chessman (king) and describing its moves.

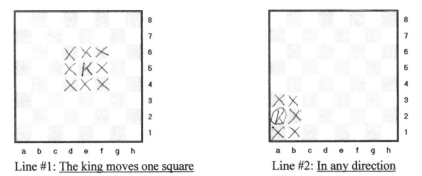

Line #1: <u>The king moves one square</u>   Line #2: <u>In any direction</u>

The blank diagrams below are for you to show your chessman's moves. Make one diagram for a white chessman and one for a black chessman. Since white and black chessmen move the same, have one chessman in the center of the board and one on the edge for variety. Use Xs to show legal moves. Under each diagram, write the two lines of lyrics for your chessman.

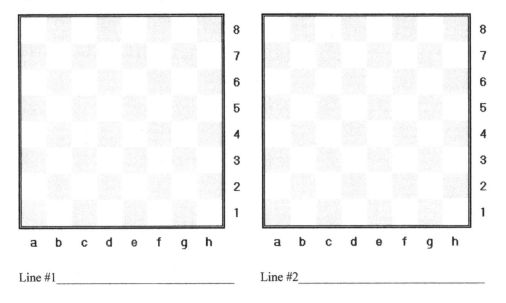

Line #1_____   Line #2_____

Figure 2.1.
Favorite chessman lyrics and diagrams.

music and theater, is by Royston (2006). "The music of the night" inspired the pun (night/knight) in this activity's title.

Procedure. For children unfamiliar with chess moves, teach step one, then step two. Repeat steps for each chessman:

Step one. Show the children a three-dimensional chessman that is used for playing and its two-dimensional counterpart from the demonstration board. Say the name of the chessman, and have children repeat its name.

Step two. On an empty demonstration board, show how that chessman moves. For example, put a white rook on a1. Show that it can move vertically along the a-file and horizontally along the first rank.

Optional: If children have room to move, play a game of Simon Says. Simon Says is a listening game in which children obey commands prefaced by the phrase "Simon Says." In my experience, even older children (ages 12–14) enjoy Simon Says. Line up the children an arm's length apart at the back of the room. Tell the children, "Simon Says to move like a rook toward the front of the room." If any children move on a **diagonal,** rather than horizontally or vertically, they are eliminated. Tell the children, "Stop." If any of them stop, they are eliminated because "Stop" was not preceded by the phrase "Simon Says." Play until you have reviewed the movements of each chessman, and then declare all children still in the game as co-winners.

Ask each child to pick another child that he or she does not know (or does not know well). Once the children are in groups of two (with one group of three if there are an odd number of children), each child asks the other, "What is your first name? What is your favorite chessman?" Then groups take turns going to the front of the room and introducing each other to the rest of the children. That is, each child introduces the child that he or she interviewed.

As introductions are being made, record which chessman each child liked. For the rest of this procedure, and for the other music activities in this chapter, children who like a particular chessman are grouped together. Adjust groups so that the number of members is the same as, or one or two over, the number of those chessmen on the board. For example, the king group may have two to four members (a white king and black king, plus one or two alternates). The knight group can have four to six members (two white knights, two black knights, and one or two alternates). The pawn group is the largest. If there are not 16 members in it, though, do not worry. Most scripts do not require 16 pawns. But every script asks for a white king and a black king, so pick consistently attending children for the king group. For *Activity Nine,* many children will choose to audition for the roles they first practiced in these music activities. If some children prefer to work independently rather than in groups, let them. For example, you might have a group working on one set of queen lyrics at the same time as an individual works on different queen lyrics.

Assemble children in their favorite-chessman groups. Each favorite-chessman group (or individual) composes two lines about their chessman. Short lines, with few syllables, work best. Each of the two lines should have about the same number of syllables. In the next activity, children will divide words into syllables and make adjustments. But mention the guidelines now, to help the composers. The song must include the following information:

1. Name of the chessman. This information must be in the first line, for example, "I am a pawn" or "I am a bishop." The line might also include some movement information. An example of a first line containing the chessman's name and movement information is "Knight moves up one and over two."
2. How the chessman moves. The second bishop line might be "Move diagonal." The second line of the knight might be "or up two over one."

Have children write their group's lyrics on Figure 2.1. Figure 2.1 also includes blank diagrams so that they might write the abbreviation of their chessman and mark (with Xs) where that chessman moves. There is one diagram to show a white chessman and one to show a black chessman. A white king's moves and a black king's moves are shown as examples on Figure 2.1, along with two lines about the king's moves. Save each group's completed Figure 2.1 for *Activity Two*. If members of one or more groups finish Figure 2.1 early, they may observe others' work on Figure 2.1

Assessment. There are several opportunities for assessment in the lesson. Are children eliminated because of chessman-moving errors or because of not paying attention to the Simon Says command? Monitor children as they complete Figure 2.1 to determine whether they know how their favorite chessman moves. Ask groups to make corrections so that their Figure 2.1 accurately names a chessman and describe its moves. Make sure the lyrics are two lines long. One group's lyrics are in Appendix A.

Activity Two: From Moves to Grooves

Content standard. Music, Content Standard 3: Improvising melodies, variations, and accompaniments.

Objectives. Children learn, or review, how the chessmen move. Children write the lyrics from *Activity One* in syllables. Children write the note values, rests, measures, and time signature of their lyrics. Children work in groups or as individuals. Children move around the room as their chessman while chanting their composition.

Resources and materials. Figure 2.1 from *Activity One*. Each child should have a pencil or pen and notebook paper. Have dictionaries available. Parents may assist groups in writing syllables and determining time signature, note values, and measure bars.

Write on the dry-erase board or photocopy Figure 2.2 (Note value, 2009) and Figure 2.3.

This chart shows some of the common note values in the 2/4, 3/4, and 4/4 time signatures (Note value, 2009).

Note symbol	Rest symbol	Name of note	2/4, 3/4, or 4/4 value
 ♩	▬	half note	two beats
 ♩	𝄾	quarter note	one beat
 ♪	𝄿	eighth note	half beat
 ♬	𝅀	sixteenth note	quarter beat

Figure 2.2.
Common note values.

Twin-kle, twin-kle, lit-tle star

1. What is the time signature?

2. What type of note is above the syllable "Twin"?

3. How many beats in a measure?

4. What type of note is above the one-syllable word "star"?

5. What does the vertical line after "kle," mean?

6. What do the two vertical lines after "star" mean?

7. Does each syllable get its own note?

8. How do you divide "twinkle" into two syllables?

Figure 2.3.
Familiar song in rhythm.

From *The Living Chess Game: Fine Arts Activities for Kids 9–14* by Alexey W. Root. Santa Barbara, CA: Libraries Unlimited. Copyright © 2011.

The activity title *From Moves to Grooves* refers to transforming words about chess moves into syllables (one syllable per note) and then grooving (moving) to a rhythmic chant about a chessman.

Procedure. Pass back Figure 2.1 to the groups (or individuals). If a small number of new children are present, integrate them into existing groups. If all the children are new, divide them into favorite-chessmen groups and offer the previously created lyrics. Or if these new children are also newcomers to chess, teach *Activity One* before beginning *Activity Two*.

To show what is expected for this activity, display Figure 2.3 by copying it on a dry-erase board or photocopying it for the children. Guide the class through the syllable division of the words and how each syllable is represented by a note. Show that some notes are held longer than others. For example, "star" is held for two beats (a half note). Chant the beginning of "Twinkle, Twinkle, Little Star," shown in Figure 2.3, together. Then have each child answer the eight questions on Figure 2.3 on his or her own before you continue with the rest of *Activity Two*. Go over the answers to Figure 2.3 (found in Appendix A) with the class.

Explain that children will divide their Figure 2.1 lines into syllables, and then figure out a time measure and beats for their composition. Pass out dictionaries or have them available at the front of the room. At the bottom of a notebook page, groups write each word of their lyrics from Figure 2.1 in syllables, for example, "I am a bish-op. Move di-ag-o-nal." Use hyphens to divide one syllable from the next. Lines should be adjusted so that each has about the same number of syllables per line. If the lines are long, have just one line at the bottom of each piece of notebook paper. Two or three pieces of notebook paper may be used.

Children assign correct note values to each syllable. The groups write the appropriate-length note above each syllable. Or vice versa is acceptable, as in Figure A.5 and Figure A.6 in Appendix A. A chart of common note values is in Figure 2.2; additional note values can be found in elementary music texts or on the Internet. One helpful site is http://www.musictheory.net/. At this point, do not worry about pitch.

Parents may help groups divide the lyrics into measures at two beats (if 2/4 time), three beats (if 3/4 time) or four beats (if 4/4 time). Indicate the time signature at the beginning of the first measure. These three time signatures are preferred because they are simple. End a measure by drawing a vertical bar line. After writing all the measures, end the composition by a double bar line.

Have children chant their composition while moving around the room as their favorite chessman. For example, a queen on an empty board may move from d1 to d8. The child portraying the queen would start chanting the first line of the queen lyrics on d1 and finish up the second line of the lyrics as he or she arrived on d8. A king on an empty board might begin the first line of the king's lyrics on e5, and then sing the second line of the king's lyrics as he or she arrives on d6. You don't need a living chess board in place for this practice. Children can imagine squares on the floor to practice their moves and chants. Collect the notes and lyrics from each group and save for use in *Activity Three*.

Assessment. Assess written lyrics for correct syllable division. Check notebook pages for the appropriate number of beats per measure, bar lines, and time signature. Examples of children's work are in Figure A.5 and Figure A.6 in Appendix A.

Activity Three: Chess in Concert

Content Standard. Music, Content Standard 5: Reading and notating music.

Objectives. Children sing a C major melody to match the rhythmic lyrics from *Activity Two*. Children write the composition using musical notation. Optional objective: If children also know chess notation, compare music and chess notation.

Resources and Materials. Lyrics on notebook paper from *Activity Two*. Each child should have a pencil or pen and staff paper. Search the Internet for "free treble clef staff paper" and print, or use the Microsoft Office Online template called "Large treble clef staff for young musicians."

Parents may provide, or play, a keyboard. Download free sheet music in the key of C. Lesson plans that meet national standards for music composition are available free online (Thomas, n.d.). Display a C major scale on the dry-erase board such as Figure 2.4. Figures 2.3, 2.4, and 2.5 were created by my 17-year-old daughter, Clarissa, accompanied by Abba the rabbit. Figure 2.6 is a photo of Clarissa at work on Figure 2.3. Display Figure 2.4 to the class, and make a copy of Figure 2.5 for each child. Figure 2.7 is chess lyrics set to the tune of "Joy to the World." Make one photocopy of Figure 2.7 for each child.

The activity title *Chess in Concert* refers to the 2009 CD and DVD release by the same name (Rice, Andersson, & Ulvaeus, 2009). That concert featured Josh Groban and the London Philharmonic, dancers performing as living chessmen, lyrics about chess, and a dramatic storyline. Having seen the musical *Chess* twice in the 1980s, I also enjoyed the DVD of *Chess in Concert*.

Procedure. If children are already familiar with chess notation (described in the section "Reading and Writing Chess" in chapter 5), then you might ask them to compare music notation and chess notation. Their answers may touch on the following points. Both music and chess notation systems allow us to record our own original compositions and games, as well as to play through those created by other musicians and chess players, past and present. Learning a new notation system is like learning a new language. After learning notation, one reads music or is literate in chess. After learning a new language, one communicates in that language.

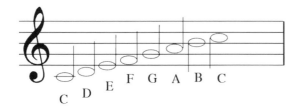

Figure 2.4.
Treble-clef C major scale with notes labeled.

Label each half note below with its note name (i.e., C, B, A, and so forth). This is a treble-clef C major scale.

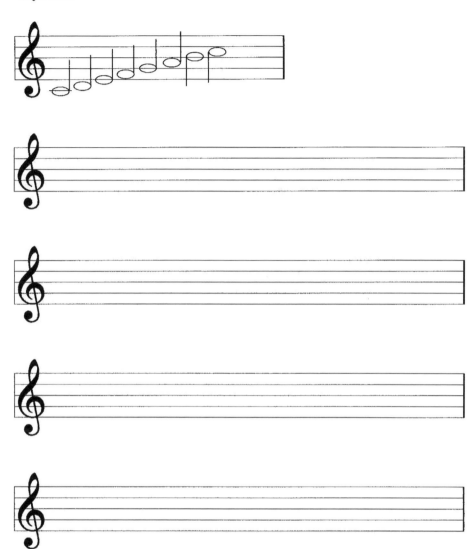

Figure 2.5.
Label the treble clef notes.

From *The Living Chess Game: Fine Arts Activities for Kids 9–14* by Alexey W. Root. Santa Barbara, CA: Libraries Unlimited. Copyright © 2011.

Figure 2.6.
Clarissa creating figures; Abba under the computer chair.

Play on the keyboard, sing, or have a parent perform the music to "Joy to the World." The first eight treble-clef notes end on middle C: C, B, A, G, F, E, D, C. Children listen to the keyboard on the first time through the music. During the second time the parent plays the music, have children sing "C, B, A, G, F, E, D, C" while looking at Figure 2.7. For the third time, while singing with the keyboard accompaniment, children again look at Figure 2.7 as they sing, "Knight moves up one and over two. Or up two over one." The time signature of "Joy to the World" is 2/4. Ask the children about the math within the time signature. The "2" on top of the time signature means there are two beats per measure. The "4" on the bottom of the time signature means that the quarter note gets the beat.

To review note values from *Activity Two,* have children write out the values for each measure of Figure 2.7. Teach or review that a dot after a note adds half again the value of the note. For example, when a quarter note is one beat, then a quarter note with a dot is one and a half beats. Measure one has a quarter note (one beat) followed by a dotted eighth note (three quarters of a beat) and a sixteenth note (one quarter of a beat). Measure two has a dotted quarter note (one and a half beats) and an eighth note (half a beat). Measure three has two quarter notes (one beat each). Measures four, five, and six each have a dotted quarter note (one and a half beats) and an eighth note (half a beat). The last measure has a half note (two beats). For an example of 4/4, play the treble-clef notes of "Twinkle, Twinkle, Little Star."

Tell children that their chessman songs will likewise use only C major treble-clef notes. Favorite-chessman groups may either borrow an existing melody (such as "Twinkle, Twinkle") or create an original C major melody. Parents may play notes in C major to assist. Or, if the keyboard is inexpensive, both children and parents can use it. Note values from *Activity Two* may be adjusted to fit melody requirements. On the same notebook paper used in *Activity Two,* groups write the tone of the note (C, D, E, F, G, A, B, or C) above the note values. The rough draft of the composition is now complete.

Display Figure 2.4 on a document viewer or on the dry-erase board. Figure 2.4 shows that note stems point up (and are on the right side of the note) for notes from middle C to the B in the middle of the treble-clef staff. Note stems point down (and are on the left) for notes above the middle of the clef. On the treble-clef staff, the B in the middle may have its note stem drawn either way. Ask children to study Figure 2.4 and ask questions

Knight moves up one and ov- er two. Or up two ov- er one.

Directions: Write the note values for each measure above and show that the values equal 2. For example, the first measure has a quarter note, dotted eighth note, and a sixteenth note. Therefore, the equation for measure one is:

1+.75+.25=2.

Or you could write the equation 1+3/4+1/4=2. On this same paper, write the equations for measures 2-7.

Figure 2.7.
Joy to the World (new lyrics).

about it. Then put it away and pass out copies of Figure 2.5 to each child. Have each child complete Figure 2.5. Tell children that the note names (C, B, A, and so forth) can be written either above the staff (as on the notebook paper rough draft) or below the staff (as in Figure 2.4). Have the children correct their work (by redisplaying Figure 2.4).

Using the beats and notes from their rough draft, groups write a final draft on staff paper. There are staff paper lines on Figure 2.5, taken from the free download from Microsoft Office "Large treble clef staff for young musicians," that can be used for the final draft. Following Thomas (n.d.), groups should plan for at least two, but no more than four, measures on each staff line. After the first treble clef, write the time signature. Then continue writing the notes and measures until the end of the composition. Remind groups to have one vertical bar line at the end of each measure and two bar lines at the end of the composition. The final step is to write the lyrics (still broken into syllables) under the staff lines and notes.

Assessment. This activity builds on work from *Activity One* and *Activity Two*. In Appendix A (Figure A.6) are the two lines of lyrics (from *Activity One*), the syllables and note values (from *Activity Two*), and the treble-clef notes (from *Activity Three*) composed by two boys, ages eight and nine. Also included in their work, from *Activity Three,* are the note values of each measure in Figure 2.7.

Evaluate the final draft for the appropriate number and value of notes per measure, correct direction of note stems, presence of measure bar lines, two to four measures per staff line, a time signature after the first treble clef, and written lyrics correctly divided into syllables under corresponding notes. An example of a 10-year-old's final draft is in Appendix A (Figure A.8).

Chapter 3

DANCE AND VISUAL ARTS

This chapter has two dance and two visual arts activities. In *Activity Four: Chess Boxing* children choreograph captures by their favorite chessman. For *Activity Five: Brains and Brawn* children practice physical and mental warm-ups, to be used before dancing or playing chess. For *Activity Six: The Art of Chess* children appreciate chess sets and boards as visual art. For *Activity Seven: All the World's a Chessboard* children borrow design ideas from the admired chess sets and boards in *Activity Six*.

Activity Four: Chess Boxing

Content standard. Dance, Content Standard 1: Identifying and demonstrating movement elements and skills in performing dance.

Objectives. Children learn, or review, how the chessmen capture. Children practice complementary actions. Children choreograph and rehearse a capture.

Resources and materials. Display Figure 3.1 on the dry-erase board or overhead projector. Have a demonstration board and one set and board.

The activity title *Chess Boxing* refers to a hybrid sport. According to the World Chess Boxing Organisation (2009), "Chessboxers go through alternating four-minute long rounds of chess and three-minute boxing rounds with a one-minute break in between" (FAQ section, para. 1). Linking chess with boxing and then boxing with dance may shatter perceptions of "sexism (that it is not masculine for boys to dance)" (Sikes, 2007, p. 58).

Add to or modify this chart with suggestions from the children. All actions should be done in slow motion, without bodily contact.

Leader's action	Responder's complementary action
Takes a small step toward responder.	Takes a small step backward.
Leans toward responder.	Leans away from leader.
Reaches arm toward responder.	Reaches opposite arm toward leader.
Throws air punch at responder.	Responder falls to the ground then exits the board.

Figure 3.1
Complementary actions.

Choreography is integral to staged boxing scenes. Sikes (2007) wrote, "For example, in the movie *Rocky,* Sylvester Stallone choreographed all of the fight sequences" (p. 61). For this activity, staged combat is stylized, suggesting a chess capture without actually making contact.

Procedure. For children unfamiliar with captures, teach step one, then step two. Repeat steps for each chessman:

Step one. Show the children a three-dimensional chessman that is used for playing and its two-dimensional counterpart from the demonstration board. Say the name of the chessman, and have children repeat its name. This step reviews information from *Activity One.*

Step two. On an empty demonstration board, show how that chessman captures. For example, put a white rook on a1. Put a black pawn on a5. Show that the rook may move from a1 to a5. When the rook arrives on a5, then the a-pawn is removed from a5. The rook remains on a5 by itself. When you demonstrate pawn captures, also teach the **en passant** rule.

Explain a complementary action. According to Barron (n.d.), the leader of the action moves freely and the responder attempts to move in a complementary fashion. Leader and responder face each other. In the living chess game, the dance occurs when a chessman's move ends on a square occupied by an enemy chessman. A leader (the chessman making a capture) and a responder (the chessman being captured) share the square during the capture dance. Their movements are in slow motion, to maximize safety and to appear stylized. Furthermore, the chessmen do not touch each other. Show children Figure 3.1.

Each capture has a beginning, a middle, and an end. The capture begins when the singing chessman (leader) arrives on the responder's square. The leader's song is from *Activity Three.* The leader finishes singing and turns to face the responder. The middle part starts when the leader makes a movement from the left column of Figure 3.1. The responder answers with a movement from the right column. The leader and responder continue complementary actions. The end is when the responder falls to the ground and then exits the board. Tell children that they may add complementary actions to Figure 3.1 or modify or eliminate actions from Figure 3.1, after practicing with a partner.

Pair up children to practice movements in Figure 3.1. They should take turns being leader and responder, both roles as chessmen. They can invent new complementary actions too. At the end of the class, have children demonstrate their captures. They should also tell what changes they made. Modify Figure 3.1 so that it includes the children's suggested complementary actions.

Assessment. Judge how much children understand by observing their participation. An additional outcome is a final draft of Figure 3.1 that includes the children's suggestions.

Activity Five: Brains and Brawn

Content standard. Dance, Content Standard 6: Making connections between dance and other disciplines.

Objectives. Children practice physical and mental warm-ups, to be used before dancing or playing chess. Children observe the effects of these warm-ups on their performances.

Resources and materials. Each child needs a pencil or pen and notebook paper. One chess set and board for every two children. The activity title is a common cultural expression about mind (brains) and body (brawn). Mind and body health are important to performing well in dance and in chess.

Procedure. Ask children why it is important to have a warm-up before dancing or playing chess. Some answers might be to prevent injury, to focus on the task ahead, and to enhance performance. Ask if dance has a mental component and if chess has a physical component. Answers should be yes. Dance requires "accurate memorization and reproduction of movement sequences" (MENC, 1994). McDonald and Fisher (2006) wrote, "In order to participate in movement and dance, students must listen, think, assimilate instructions and sequences, pattern their ideas physically, communicate and coordinate with others, become a part of a group effort, and *show* what they have learned" (p. 100, italics in original).

Chess players experience physical stress during games (Root, 2006, p. 8). **FIDE Masters, International Masters**, and **Grandmasters** train physically as well as at the board (Root, 2006, pp. 18–19). In her interview of Harvard professor, world-renowned economist, and former child chess prodigy Kenneth Rogoff, Cheng (2009) wrote:

> Because he spends so much time working and travelling, he says he needs to exercise and meditate for relaxation. "I learned this when I was playing chess. You have to have stamina for so many days and hours. You have to train and until today, although I don't play chess anymore, I continue to train." (last para.)

As a whole group, children try one physical and one mental warm-up created by experts in dance and chess. Ask children to pay attention to what effect (if any) the warm-up has on their subsequent performance.

Say and demonstrate each step of the physical warm-up while children copy you. The physical warm-up is from Stacy Elise Stevenson (n.d.), a performing arts educator at Carl Sandburg Middle School in Alexandria, Virginia:

> The following is a good example of a basic warm-up procedure (each movement should be repeated several times):

> - Roll the head gently, nodding up and down, then looking side to side.
> - Slowly roll the shoulders forward, then backward.

- Circle the arms forward, then backwards. Swing the arms.
- Twist the upper body at the waist, then bend side to side, and forwards and backwards.
- Rotate the hips clockwise, then counterclockwise.
- Bend the knees deeply.
- Shake out the legs, one at a time.
- Roll each ankle in circles, clockwise and counterclockwise.
- Stretch the whole body, rising on toes and stretching the arms toward the ceiling.
- Shake out the whole body.

Now ask the children to capture as their favorite chessman, as in *Activity Four.* Have a class discussion about whether the children felt differently capturing because they participated in the warm-up.

For the mental warm-up, ask children to sit still. Closing their eyes may help them concentrate on this mental warm-up. Read aloud each part of the warm-up by Dr. Leo Stefurak (2004), president of the Chess Mates Foundation and a chess **master.** Boldface added to Stefurak's warm-up to indicate glossary entries.

To succeed at chess create and sustain the following positive imagery:

1. See yourself playing slowly and deliberately
2. See your eyes scanning the chessboard looking for opportunities
3. See yourself looking for **checks**, captures and threats on every move
4. See yourself finding a good move . . . and then seeking for a better one
5. See yourself sitting quietly at your board thinking
6. See yourself finding the flaw in your opponent's play
7. Hear your mind constructing a **variation**
8. Hear your pieces quietly talking to you
9. See your pieces moving around to different squares on their own
10. See your pieces just beaming over to their best square
11. See yourself getting tough when the going gets tough
12. Hear yourself questioning the accuracy of your opponent's move
13. When you are winning, see the pieces being traded off
14. When in trouble, see yourself setting up obstacles for your opponent
15. See your pieces working together and making something good happen
16. See yourself watching yourself and listening to yourself during play
17. See yourself moving at a slow, steady pace which you set yourself
18. See yourself remaining emotionally calm during play
19. See your mind reaching out and making an effort on every move
20. See yourself being gracious in victory and silent in defeat

Pair up the children to play a chess game, passing out one set and board for every two children. As children complete their games, have each child write a few sentences about the effect of the warm-up on his or her performance in that game.

Assessment. Listen to the class discussion after the physical warm-up and capture movements, and read the sentences after the chess games. Appendix A has a few sentences from an eight-year-old about the effect of the mental warm-up on his subsequent chess game.

Activity Six: The Art of Chess

Content standard. Visual Arts, Content Standard 5: Reflecting upon and assessing the characteristics and merits of their work and the work of others.

Objectives. Children appreciate chess sets and boards as visual art. Children write an art critique that includes description, analysis, interpretation, and judgment. Children share their critiques with each other.

Resources and materials. Find photos of artistically designed chess sets and boards in books such as List (2005), Schafroth (2002), or Williams (2000). Photocopy pages that show chessmen, boards, or both. Or use the Internet. Some online choices are Shahade (2009) and Fitch (2006). Print photos from those Web sites, or have the sites displayed on computer monitors. If you or the children own unique chess sets and boards, bring those in for this activity. Have at least one set (or photo or photocopy of a set) per child in class; best is two or three per child. In this activity, the word "set" refers to either a three-dimensional set (or set and board) or a photo or photocopy of a three-dimensional set (or set and board).

The activity title *The Art of Chess* refers to two books with that title. The more recent, about chess, art, and the artist Marcel Duchamp, is Nauman, Bailey, and Shahade (2009). The older one, Schafroth (2002), connects chess set design to historical place and time.

R. G. Meyer (2002) is my Internet source for the art critiquing process in Figure 3.2. Photocopy Figure 3.2, one copy for each child, and make one copy for an overhead projector.

Procedure. Have artistic chess sets on display. For example, put three sets on each long table. Or, if you have desks, put one set on every two pushed-together desks. Allow children to walk around the room to look at each set. The room is thus configured as an art gallery. Ask children to sit next to the set that they wish to critique, as long as not more than one other child has picked that set. This rule evenly distributes the children among the tables (or desks) and chairs.

Pass out Figure 3.2. As you read aloud through each part on the overhead copy of Figure 3.2, each child fills out each part (description, analysis, interpretation, and judgment). Explain, and answer any questions about, the meanings of different terms. For example, you might explain how to find the name of the artist. Or you may need to tell what proportion is. You may walk around the room to point out parts of the sets.

After all children have filled out Figure 3.2, ask them to place their completed Figure 3.2 papers next to their sets. Then children walk through

Directions: For the chess set that you selected, fill in the blanks for description, analysis, interpretation, and judgment.

Description: If available, tell the name of the artist, the name of the set, and the year created. Then describe what the set looks like. _____

_____

_____

Analysis: Some elements of art (line, shape, space, form, texture, value, and color) and principles of design (balance, proportion, rhythm & movement, emphasis & variety, harmony & unity) may apply. At minimum, identify forms (three-dimensional figures), colors, and proportion (how does the king compare to the pawn? How does each chessman fit on its square?).

_____

_____

_____

_____

Interpretation: What was the artist saying to the people who might play on the set and board? What elements of art or principles of design help get his message across?

_____

_____

_____

Judgment: What do you think about this chess set and board? Would you display it in your home? Would you use it for playing chess?

_____

_____

_____

_____

Figure 3.2
Art critique form.

From *The Living Chess Game: Fine Arts Activities for Kids 9–14* by Alexey W. Root. Santa Barbara, CA: Libraries Unlimited. Copyright © 2011.

Figure 3.3.
Filling out Figure 3.2 while looking at chess set.

the room to read each other's Figure 3.2s, especially the judgment part. Finally, have children stand next to the set that they like best. There will probably be at least two or three sets that have more children next to them than the other sets. Save those two or three favorite artistic sets for *Activity Seven*. Or if sets need to be returned, select the class favorite now.

Assessment. Review the answers the children have written for Figure 3.2. Keep the sets (or photos or photocopies of those sets) that were the class favorites. For *Activity Seven,* those will inspire costume and scenery design. A 10-year-old child's answers for Figure 3.2, about the chess set in Figure 3.3, are in Appendix A.

Activity Seven: All the World's a Chessboard

Content Standard. Visual Arts, Content Standard 2: Using knowledge of structures and functions.

Objectives. Children borrow theatrical design ideas from their class's favorite set and board from *Activity Six.*

Resources and Materials. The essay "Design and Production" (Arts-Alive.ca, 2009) provides definitions, information, and activities for teachers and students exploring costume and set (scenery/stage) design. The activity title is a paraphrase from Shakespeare's *As You Like It*:

> All the world's a stage,
> And all the men and women merely players.

The world of the living chess game is a chessboard. This activity has children, parents, and staff designing that stage.

Determine where the children will perform living chess game, as that information is necessary for this activity's procedure. Children need pen or pencil, as well as blank paper, colored pencils, and rulers. Provide a shoebox or other receptacle for comments and scratch paper for those comments.

Procedure. Tell the children where the living chess game will be performed. Discuss how the view of the audience influences set and costume design. If the audience will be seated above the actors, as in the bleachers of a gym, then a chessboard pattern on the floor makes the actors' chess moves clear. Hats and crowns might distinguish the chessmen from each other. If the audience will not see the stage floor, because it is seated at the same level or below the actors, then use a PowerPoint projection (on a screen behind the actors) of the game's moves. Or have a demonstration

Pawns in their own game

Kids learn chess, theater at North Branch Library

Participants are learning more than how to play chess in the Living Chess Game class at North Branch Library.

The 12-week program has also been teaching youngsters about the various aspects of a musical theater performance. The program ends with a performance Tuesday.

The children helped write the show's songs and script, chose the theme for the performance and decided how the living chess pieces would move.

"This is mainly a show that has been created by these students," said program instructor Alexey Root.

Root, a former high school teacher and 1999 U.S. women's chess champion, now uses her chess skills to promote learning.

She has hosted chess clubs at area schools and has written books on using chess as tool to teach children other skills. This group consists of home-schooled children ages 7-14.

Throughout the course, Root introduced participants to a variety of themed chess sets — from the more traditional to the more contemporary, she said.

The students chose to re-create the Super Mario Bros. Chess Set for their presentation.

The Living Chess Game performance will be at 4 p.m. Tuesday at North Branch Library, 3020 N. Locust St.

For more information, call 940-349-8752.

— Rachel Mehlhaff

Courtesy photo
Two participants of the Living Chess Game at North Branch Library pose recently in front of a poster advertising their finale at 4 p.m. Tuesday.

EVENTS
Continued from Page 2

TUESDAY

Noon to 5 p.m. — **"Faces and Mazes,"** an exhibition by Lia Cook, is on display at the UNT Art Gallery, 1201 W. Mulberry St.

1 to 5 p.m. — **"Storybook Quilts,"** a Denton Quilt Guild exhibit, is in the Meadows Gallery at the Center for the Visual Arts, 400 E. Hickory St. Free. Visit www.dentonarts.com or call 940-382-2787.

4 p.m. — **Living Chess Game** presentation at North Branch Library, 3020 N. Locust St. Free. Call 940-484-2265 or e-mail alexeyroot @gmail.com.

8 p.m. — **Trombonist John Mосса**

Figure 3.4
Denton Record-Chronicle article.

From *The Living Chess Game: Fine Arts Activities for Kids 9–14* by Alexey W. Root. Santa Barbara, CA: Libraries Unlimited. Copyright © 2011.

board, and a narrator to show chess moves on it, hanging at the eye level of the audience.

Discuss whether the designs of the favorite sets would show up well in the planned performance space, Then, as a group, vote on the class's favorite set and board from *Activity Six*. (A favorite set and board might already have been picked at the end of *Activity Six*). This favorite set and board becomes the basis of the group's living chess game theatrical show. Discuss whether some set and board elements and principles, such as particular colors or proportions, might be used in the show's design. Make a list on the dry-erase board of these elements and principles. Depending on the set selected, chessmen actors might wear T-shirts (lighter color for the white chessmen) decorated with an image of their piece or pawn. Or they might carry props, or wear makeup, to indicate their roles. Nonmoving chessmen might be represented by decorated chairs. The two actors cast as the players of the living chess game might wear period costumes.

Divide children into groups. If possible, assign a parent or staff person to groups for makeup, T-shirts and period costumes, hats or crowns, props, set decorations, publicity (posters, flyers, and T-shirts advertising the show), and set design. Remind groups to incorporate the elements on the dry-erase board. Ask each group to either write their ideas on scratch paper or sketch those ideas using the blank paper and colored pencils.

Assessment. As each group completes its work, post that group's written ideas and sketches on a bulletin board. Be sure to clearly label each group's efforts with a group name, such as "Makeup." Put a shoe box and scratch paper near the bulletin board. Invite those that finish earlier than others to write comments about the bulletin board work. Then they place those comments in the shoebox. Remind children to refer to the elements and principles on the dry-erase board in their comments. Appendix A shows a publicity poster drawn by a nine-year-old. That publicity-poster photo also appeared in the *Denton Record-Chronicle*'s article about the living chess game performance at the Denton Public Library (Mehlhaff, 2009). A photocopy is in Figure 3.4.

Chapter 4

THEATER

The first four activities in this chapter prepare for a living chess game performance. In *Activity Eight: Immortal and Evergreen* children write a script. First, they study a famous chess game or problem corresponding to the number of actors in their class. The script incorporates prior work from *Activity Three* (musical themes for the moves of chessmen) and *Activity Four* (choreography to represent the chessmen's captures). In *Activity Nine: No Small Parts* children audition by performing excerpts from *Activity Eight*'s script. Most children will be cast as living chessmen. One or two actors will annotate (narrate) the living chess game. For *Activity Ten: Tech and Check* children, staff, and parent volunteers collaboratively create scenery, costumes, and makeup based on designs from *Activity Seven*. For *Activity Eleven: The Living Chess Game* children first use warm-ups from *Activity Five* or other warm-ups that you have chosen for them. For the first rehearsal, children sit in a circle and read through the script together. For subsequent rehearsals, children rehearse the living chess game. After rehearsals are completed, the children perform for an audience. *Activity Twelve: Talent Show* is a stand-alone activity. A talent show allows children to rehearse, perform, and evaluate fine arts performances.

Activity Eight: Immortal and Evergreen

Content standard. Theater, Content Standard 1: Script writing by the creation of improvisations and scripted scenes based on personal experience and heritage, imagination, literature, and history.

Objectives. Children research a chess game or problem and imagine the thoughts and emotions experienced by white or black. Children write dialogue or create facial expressions based on those thoughts and emotions.

Resources and materials. Each child should have a pencil or pen and notebook paper. Each child should also have a highlighter pen. If going over background material as a whole group, have a demonstration board available. From Appendix C, pick a chess game or problem that corresponds to the number of children in class. Then, for each child, make one photocopy of its algebraic notation. Separately provide photocopies with background material about the players (or composer) and annotations. Display Figure 4.1 on the overhead projector or copy it onto a dry-erase board. You will fill in Figure 4.1 with responses from the children. For every two children, one chess set and board. Optional: Photocopies of Figure 4.2 if children will write the script.

The activity title *Immortal and Evergreen* refers to two of the most famous games in chess history, the Immortal and the Evergreen. Both can be found in Appendix C. Appendix C has five examples of chess games and problems. For more choices, search for any short (less than 25 moves long) chess game or chess problem. Best are games with moves by different chessmen or with several captures, as that makes for an exciting living chess game. Such chess games and chess problems can be found on the Internet or by browsing through chess books.

If children write the script, adult help and more time is required. If you are writing the script, you may stop the lesson before the optional portion of the procedure.

Procedure. Tell children to imagine themselves as either white or black in a chess game or problem. As they play through the moves they should write down what they are feeling or thinking and make a related facial expression. As an example give the thought and emotion, "After 10. Rxd8, I just lost my black queen! I feel terrible." Make a sad face.

Give the algebraic notation of the selected chess game or problem to every child. Then pair children and pass out a chess set and board to each pair. Ask each pair to play through the moves and to write what one side was likely feeling or thinking on at least five different moves. They may also include expressions (draw emoticons) such as smiling, frowning, and so forth. Make sure some of the pairs are writing about white and some are writing about black.

Reconvene the children as a whole class after 15–20 minutes. With their responses, fill in Figure 4.1 as you display it on the overhead projector or dry-erase board. Then either pass out photocopies of the background material and the annotated game or problem or go over that material as a whole group. If reconvening the pairs, ask them to play through the game again while reading the background material and annotations. Ask each child to mark with a highlighter pen which parts of the background material and annotations belong in the script. This will take another 15–20 minutes. A quicker alternative is to review the background material as a

Move, i.e., 1. e4 or 1. . . . e5	What white felt or thought. Optional: Include facial expression such as ☹	What black felt or thought. Optional: Include facial expression such as ☺

Figure 4.1.
From notation to narration.

From *The Living Chess Game: Fine Arts Activities for Kids 9–14* by Alexey W. Root. Santa Barbara, CA: Libraries Unlimited. Copyright © 2011.

Here are some tips for writing your script:

- If typing on a word processor, use Courier font as shown in this figure. Put the name of the play and the names of the authors on a title page.
- On the page following the title page, list the chessmen and narrator parts in the play. Include which chessmen will be portrayed by props. For example,

Character name	Prop or actor
WHITE PAWN (a-file)	Actor
WHITE PAWN (b-file)	Prop
ANDERSSEN	Actor

This page should also state that this is a one-act play with no intermission.

- The next page describes the setting in italics. For example,

  On the chessboard stage are living chessmen and props in the starting position of a chess game. Near the chessboard are two players, ANDERSSEN and DUFRESNE.

  After establishing the setting, continue on the same page with the beginning of the play, that is, the dialogue or action.
- A character's name is always written in capital letters. For your script, characters might include MORPHY and COUNT ISOUARD.
- Dialogue for the character follows a colon, and begins on the left of the page. As a new character speaks, a new line begins. For example,

ANDERSSEN: I am from Germany.
DUFRESNE: I am your chess student, but I will try to win against you in our game.

- Words that should be stressed or said more clearly are underlined, for example,

ANDERSSEN: I am the best player in the world.

The chessmen are nonspeaking characters, but they may have actions or stage movements.

Actions and stage movements are written in italics. For example,

10. axb4, and the other black chessmen's faces show dismay.

Which is shorthand in the script for the following:

On white's 10th move, the WHITE PAWN (a-file) sings as it moves from a3 to b4. The WHITE PAWN and BLACK BISHOP (on b4) dance using complementary actions. The WHITE PAWN captures the BLACK BISHOP. When that happens, the other black chessmen's faces show dismay.

- Entrances and exits are written in brackets. For example, the previous stage movement 10. axb4 also implies the following exit: [The captured BLACK BISHOP exits the stage.] Since this exit is implied, do not write it. But you may have other occasions to include in the script an entrance or an exit, such as [DUFRESNE exits the stage.].
- If there is an action within dialogue, use italics and parentheses to set off the action. For example,

MORPHY: *(scowling)* Why are we playing chess during an opera?

Figure 4.2.
Dialogue and action in a sample script.

From *The Living Chess Game: Fine Arts Activities for Kids 9–14* by Alexey W. Root. Santa Barbara, CA: Libraries Unlimited. Copyright © 2011.

whole group, with you moving the chessmen on the demonstration board. In that case, highlight on the background photocopies the material that the children believe belongs in the script.

Optional: Depending on the sophistication of the children and the time available, they may write the script. The action and stage movements of the chessmen may remain as algebraic notation. When the notation indicates a move, there will be the music and movement previously worked out in *Activity Three*. When the notation shows a capture, there will additionally be a movement sequence as in *Activity Four*. Therefore, writing the players' or composer's narrative dialogue is the main task. Facial expressions may also be included in the script. Pass out Figure 4.2 to the script writers for guidance, along with the highlighted copies of the background material and annotations.

Parent help would be welcome for script writing. It may be best if a small group of children volunteer for script writing, as it is easier to get consensus in a small group. At the same time that these children and their parent helpers are writing, other children may volunteer for set building (see *Activity Ten*).

Assessment. When children play through the algebraic notation, judge whether their writing reflects what white or black might have been thinking or feeling. Are their comments similar to the annotations in Appendix C? Appendix A gives an example of a completed Figure 4.1.

Next, when the children highlight the background material and annotations, are they doing so with understanding? Ask, "Why did you highlight this particular annotation?" Or if discussing the background material as a whole group, are the children attentive? Do they make relevant comments?

If children write a script, determine if they followed the guidelines in Figure 4.2. A script written by 13 children, ages 9–13, is in Appendix A. In addition to a living chess game, the script includes a preshow where children show off their dance (capture) moves in pairs and groups.

Activity Nine: No Small Parts

Content standard. Theater, Content Standard 2: Acting by assuming roles and interacting in improvisations.

Objectives. Children catalog their past theatrical experiences, physical dimensions, and contact information. They list their availability for rehearsals and performance. Children demonstrate acting skills (such as sensory recall, concentration, breath control, diction, body alignment, control of isolated body parts) to develop characterizations that suggest artistic choices.

Resources and materials. The director of the play should have copies (one copy per actor) of an audition form such as Figure 4.3. Children need a pencil or pen for filling out their information. Add your specific dates and information to Figure 4.3.

AUDITIONS and CREW INTERVIEWS

for the play

_____ (title of play)

When? _____

Where? _____

How? Sign up for an audition/interview slot at _____

Play Synopsis: This one-act play consists of narration (by one or more actors) and chess moves by several more actors portraying living chessmen. The living chessmen parts are not speaking parts, but require singing and dancing. The narrator parts are speaking parts only. There may also be an opportunity for a preshow, where pairs or groups of children demonstrate chess music and dance. You may sign up for a crew role in addition to your acting role or roles. Please indicate later in this form which acting and crew roles interest you.

Crew Roles: Costumes, Properties, Publicity, Makeup, Set Construction, Stage Crew, and

_____

Questions? E-mail _____ or call _____

Please select one monologue, song, or dance for your audition. For the singing audition, you are encouraged to sing the lyrics and music created for a chessman's move. You may show movement or sing standing still. If you plan a dance audition, you may audition with a partner to show complementary actions for a chess capture. Or you may audition solo by moving from one square to another to another (as a particular chessman moves, with singing optional). Select a monologue audition only if you are trying out for one of the narrator (chess player or chess composer) parts.

Fill out the following information and turn in to the director before your audition:

Name _____

Age _____

School _____ Grade _____

E-mail _____

Home Phone _____

Cell Phone _____

Height _____ Weight _____

In which acting, dancing, or singing role or roles are you interested?

_____

In which crew role or roles are you interested?

_____

Will you accept any role in this play? (Circle one) Yes   No

On the back of this page, list any conflicts that you have with our proposed rehearsal times. Please note that all cast and crew members must be available _____ for technical rehearsals and performances. You are expected to be at all scheduled rehearsals. If you cannot attend a rehearsal because of illness or emergency circumstances, contact _____ _____. Children with lateness or absenteeism may be recast or asked to leave the production.

Some costume pieces, makeup, and properties may be supplied by children.

_____

Child's Signature

For Parents/Guardians

E-mail ____

Home Phone ____

Cell Phone ____

_________Please check if you would like to volunteer to help with the production.

My child, ____________________________, has permission to participate in the ____________ ____________________according to the dates listed on the audition form. It is the responsibility of the child's parent/guardian to provide transportation home promptly at the conclusion of rehearsals.

Signature of parent/guardian ____

Printed name of parent/guardian ____

____

Director's area:

Audition notes ____

____

The child was cast as ____

Crew role ____

Figure 4.3.
Audition form.

Figure 4.3 was adapted from http://www.parkridge.k12.nj.us/SBuckley/Middle%20School%20Play/SA%20 AUDITIONS.doc.

The activity title refers to the quote by Milan Kundera, available on multiple Web sites: "There are no small parts. Only small actors." Have a parent volunteer available to play a DVD or CD such as *Chess in Concert* (Rice, Andersson, & Ulvaeus, 2009) for those waiting for their auditions. Or ask the volunteer to supervise children who are filling out Figure 4.3 late or who are practicing for their auditions.

Procedure. Write the Milan Kundera quote "There are no small parts. Only small actors" on the dry-erase board. Discuss the quote with the children. Some children will take the quote literally, thinking that it refers to tiny actors. Explain instead that every role can be played expansively, and each part is important. Just as in chess, every piece and pawn has an important role. In some games, a pawn (by checkmating or by **promoting**) is actually the key player. State what you look for when you cast roles, such as concentration, staying in character, a clear voice, and distinct movements. Tell the children that they will be signing up for auditions and pass out the Figure 4.3 forms. Inform children that the form needs to be filled out and then returned at the audition.

At the audition, have children first do the warm-ups from *Activity Five*. If there will be a group of children waiting to audition, ask a parent volunteer to monitor them. Perhaps the volunteer might play a chess-themed DVD or CD, such as *Chess in Concert* (Rice, Andersson, & Ulvaeus, 2009), supervise late-filling-out of Figure 4.3, or allow practicing for auditions. Children might also audition for a preshow demonstration of particular chessmen's moves and captures. The preshow gives children more performance choices. For example, a child fond of a song he or she wrote for the activities in chapter 2 can sing that in the preshow, but be a narrator (nonsinging role) for the main living chess game. The sample script in Appendix A includes a preshow.

Assessment. Use Figure 4.3 to make notes about each child's audition. There is a space for your notes after the parent form. Cast the play based on results from the children's auditions.

Activity Ten: Tech and Check

Content standard. Theater, Content Standard 3: Designing by developing environments for improvised and scripted scenes.

Objectives. Children develop focused ideas for the environment using visual elements (such as color and texture) and visual principles (such as proportion and unity). Children work collaboratively and safely to select and create elements of scenery, property, costumes, and makeup to suggest character.

Resources and materials. Figure 4.4 lists some options for creating the chessboard scenery. Using the parent volunteer information on Figure 4.3, contact parents for help for this activity. Have parents donate materials, including new art supplies. You may also contact others for help. A church donated a living chess board to Hedrick Elementary School, Lewisville,

Options for creating a chessboard-patterned stage

Product and Location	Advantages	Disadvantages
Sidewalk chalk on an outdoor asphalt or concrete surface.	Bucket of 20 large pieces of sidewalk chalk $2.50; buy 3–4 buckets. Easy for children to use.	Will wash away in rain. Performance has to be outdoors.
Spray paint on grass.	Can of spray paint that is safe for grass $4.00; buy at least two cans. Long-lasting; will not wash away in rain.	Adults have to spray paint, because of inhalation hazard (Gelineau, 2004, p. 54). Performance has to be outdoors.
White butcher paper, crayons/ markers, scissors, and masking tape on indoor floor.	Roll of butcher paper $25; 100 crayons and markers $15; roll of masking tape $5; several pairs of scissors $5. Will be leftover supplies for other projects. Easy for children to use.	May tear when stepped on. Will last for only one performance. May not be allowed to tape butcher paper down on certain floors, such as gymnasium floors.
Painter drop cloths (painted) on indoor floor.	Box of six 4' by 5' heavy-duty canvas drop cloths $25; can of primer paint (white) $25; can of dark paint $25; paintbrushes $10. Drop cloths should be relatively stable on floor. Can be used for multiple performances.	Adults must paint the drop cloths, due to possible paint hazard for children (Gelineau, 2004, pp. 54–55).
Commercially produced giant-sized chessboards.	Can be purchased with chessmen, so may be used as giant chess set when not in use for living chess game. Extremely durable.	Limited color and style selection. Will cost several hundred dollars.

Figure 4.4.
Materials for chessboard scenery.

Texas. For his Eagle Scout project, a high school boy raised money for Hedrick's living chess game costumes and spearheaded construction of adjoining tables and benches (Bever, 2009). Avoid used or repackaged art supplies, as those may have toxic ingredients (Gelineau, 2004, p. 55). From parents and other sources, gather costumes, makeup, items from Figure 4.4, poster boards, light and dark T-shirts. You may already have a bulletin board of sketches from *Activity Seven,* where children came up with their ideas for costumes, makeup, and set design. Post or retrieve those sketches now.

I assume that you will not have special lighting or sound (microphones) for your living chess game. But if you plan for light and sound, then work on those projects during this activity. Some children may volunteer for tech work, either because they prefer it to script writing (*Activity Eight*) or because they marked a crew job on their audition form (*Activity Nine*). For this activity, a small group of children and several parents is ideal.

The activity title refers to the technical side of theater or "tech." "Check" is a term from chess. "Check" also means to inspect or test out, an important part of safety in set construction.

Procedure. Display the sketches from *Activity Seven.* Ask children to find sketches (of costumes, makeup, sets, etc.) that have unity. That is, there should be similar colors, proportions, and textures found in the selected sketches. As Gelineau (2004) wrote, "Repeating elements in an art composition can bring unity to the work, giving the viewer the feeling that everything seen belongs together" (p. 40). Children may debate and vote on which sketches belong together.

Once there is a unified vision, much will depend on the materials and time available. You can divide the children and parents into teams, with one team working on costumes, one on makeup, one on constructing the scenery, and so forth. There could also be a team to work on posters, T-shirts, or other publicity for the show.

Ideally, claim a dedicated performance space so that you do not have to dismantle the teams' work every day. For example, store costumes and makeup in a dressing room. The chessboard (set construction) could be left in process on the stage.

Assessment. Listen to the children as they decide on a unified concept for the production. Do they refer to visual art concepts learned in *Activities Six* and *Seven?* At the end of the activity, has the necessary tech work (preparation for dress rehearsals) been accomplished? Figure 4.5 shows the chessboard created by Tracy Fisher, MOSAIC director, for the August 3–7, 2009, camp. She used painter drop cloths. Each of the 64 squares was 25 inches square.

Figure 4.5.
Costumes and scenery for a living chess game.

The 9–10:30 A.M. August 2009 class in Figure 4.5 had pawns kneel, based on the Chinese chess set in Figure 3.3. In the foreground of Figure 4.5 is a black pawn on h5 and a white king on h8. In the background, seated off the board, is a white queen in waiting. The white pawn is kneeling on c6. In the far background, on a6, is the black king (wearing a white shirt with dark sleeves). This is the starting position for the Réti endgame in Appendix C.

Activity Eleven: The Living Chess Game

Content standard. Theater, Content Standard 4: Directing by organizing rehearsals for improvised and scripted scenes.

Objectives. For the first rehearsal, children read through the script in a circle that contains the director (instructor) and all the actors (children). Children lead small groups in planning visual and aural elements and in rehearsing improvised and scripted scenes, demonstrating social, group, and consensus skills.

Resources and materials. Each child should have a copy of the script and a pencil. Copies of Figure 4.6 or other rehearsal evaluation form, for use by you and others at selected rehearsals. Figure 4.6 is adapted from Haley (2008).

The activity title refers to chess games where chessmen are portrayed by human actors. Living chess games in Marostica, Italy, and Ströbeck, Germany, are famous tourist attractions.

Parent help during rehearsals—such as assisting the child directors, playing the keyboard, or assisting with technical aspects—is welcome. Parents may also be needed backstage during the performances. Parents, family members, and friends should be in the audience for the performances. If you have a small number of children, or no parent volunteers, you may rehearse all children together rather than separately.

Procedure. Start each rehearsal by having the children perform the warm-ups from *Activity Five* or other warm-ups that you have chosen for them. For the first rehearsal only, have children sit in a circle with copies of the script and a pencil for each of them. Read through the script together, answering questions and correcting any errors. This procedure is known as a read-through or table-read. The director (instructor) should also sit in the circle and make any changes or corrections needed in the script. For example, if a narrator cannot read one of his or her lines, modify that line. Living chessmen either talk or sing through their songs but do not move or dance through them during the table-read. Sometime after the table-read, photocopy corrected copies of the script for subsequent rehearsals.

For early rehearsals after the table-read, if the number of children and volunteers allows, divide the children into four groups: the narrators, who are the players or the composer; the white chessmen; the black chessmen; and four child directors. The child directors will likely also be actors in the group they direct. For example, the director for the white chessmen

Dimensions	1 Needs Improvement	2 On Your Way	3 Way to Go	4 You Nailed It	Score (1-4)
Preparation	Performance not memorized, minimal application in rehearsal.	Performance somewhat memorized, more rehearsal needed.	Performance mostly memorized, rehearsal time could increase.	Performance memorized and sufficiently rehearsed.	
Focus	Minimal concentration and connection. Generalized interpretation.	Somewhat concentrated but little connection to character. Needs more attention to specifics.	Concentration consistent but not always present in character. Somewhat generalized performance.	Consistent concentration and believability in character. Keen attention to specifics.	
Story	Uses inappropriate language, has minimal understanding of story and limited execution.	Sometimes uses inappropriate language, has limited comprehension and execution of story line	Usually presents appropriate language and complete understanding of story, execution not always connected.	Consistent use of appropriate language, full understanding and execution of story line.	
Interpretation	Minimal believability, rarely achieves author's intent, no research evident.	Sometimes clear in objectives, tone, and believability. Limited research.	Consistent believability and clear in objectives, choices reflect some research.	Almost always presents believability and clear objectives in author's tone and intent, choices reflect research.	
Physical and Vocal Characterization	Minimal expression of ideas through voice and movement, dialogue seems unconnected.	Sometimes expresses ideas with movement and voice, needs to more make creative choices.	Ideas somewhat expressed through creative movements and vocal choices. Presence mostly consistent.	Expresses ideas consistently through creative and suitable movement and vocal choices. Presence remains consistent.	
Overall Performance	Minimal sense of ensemble, no connection to others. Limited and inappropriate use of props and costumes.	Limited sense of ensemble and connection to others. Some-times uses props and costumes correctly.	Somewhat consistent sense of ensemble and interaction. Knowledge of uses of props and costumes.	Consistent sense of ensemble and interaction with others. Imaginative use of props and costumes.	

Your Grade _____ Date _____

Figure 4.6.
Rehearsal and performance evaluation form.

likely also has a role as a white chessman. One child director might work with the narrators on rehearsing his or her lines. Two other child directors should work separately with the white and black chessmen on their movements (see *Activity Three*). A child musical director should be available to rehearse the songs from *Activity Three*. Have a keyboard or tuner available to make sure actors stay in the key of C.

After rehearsing the white and black chessmen separately, the chessmen directors should cooperate to rehearse the captures from *Activity Four*. Designating each chessman's moves and captures is called blocking, a technical term for the basic broad movements of an actor on stage. Actors will incorporate details, such as facial expressions, for when bad or good moves happen for their side.

Later in the rehearsal schedule, the narrators and chessmen also need technical rehearsals together, where the play is performed in order. At this point, you (the adult in charge) may want to run the rehearsals. That way, the actor-directors can concentrate on their acting roles. Or a child who has enjoyed directing, and is not needed for an acting role, can become the stage manager for the performances of the play.

Assessment. Use Figure 4.6 or a similar form to evaluate children during rehearsals and, optionally, on the performance day. For Figure 4.6 to be most useful to children, be sure to evaluate at an early rehearsal, and then again during a midpoint rehearsal. That way, children can see where they have improved and where they still need work. Invite other adults, perhaps theater directors at a local middle school or community theater, to watch rehearsals and give feedback. They might also fill out Figure 4.6 for your performers.

Activity Twelve: Talent Show

Content standard. Theater, Content Standard 6: Comparing and incorporating art forms by analyzing methods of presentation and audience response for theatre, dramatic media (such as film, television, and electronic media), and other art forms.

Objectives. Children incorporate elements of dance, music, and visual arts to express ideas and emotions in products and performances. Children express and compare personal reactions to several art forms.

Resources and materials. Before the audition date, children and teachers should become familiar with Figure 4.7. On the audition day, judges (who may be teachers or children or both) should have a copy of Figure 4.7 to fill out for each solo or group performance (live act). If more live acts audition than there are time slots available for the talent show, select the highest-scoring acts to be in the talent show.

On audition day, the teacher should check the artwork's appropriateness for its intended audience. The teacher should assess (on audition day and before) whether effort went in to the artist's creation. If the artwork meets those standards, include it. Since artwork doesn't take up talent show

Fill out separate form for each GROUP or for each SOLOIST.

Name of performance _____

Students in group (list all their names here):

_____

_____

_____

Audition points awarded:

+_____ (fill in number of students in the group, that is, fill in 3 if there are three members in group)

+_____ (fill in 1 here if you can see faces of performers)

+_____ (fill in 1 here if you can hear the performers)

+_____ (fill in 1 here if at least one performer demonstrates artistic excellence)

+_____ (fill in 1 here if all the performers seem coordinated with each other)

_____ [Subtotal points; that is, add up previous five spaces above]

−_____ (subtract one point for every minute over three minutes)

_____ **TOTAL POINTS**

Groups (or soloists) with the highest **TOTAL POINTS** will be selected for the talent show.

Figure 4.7.
Evaluation form.

From *The Living Chess Game: Fine Arts Activities for Kids 9–14* by Alexey W. Root. Santa Barbara, CA: Libraries Unlimited. Copyright © 2011.

time, make space for multiple artworks to encourage all children to be a part of the talent show. Many children may be too shy to perform live acts but may submit an artwork.

If selecting talent show winners is a goal, create ballots. Ballots can be as simple as first choice, second choice, and third choice for live performances and for visual artwork. Distribute the ballots to audience members on talent show day so that each may anonymously rank the live acts and the artwork. Winners of the live acts and of the artworks can be announced after ballots are tallied. Parents might help with rehearsing children, donating costumes or materials, crew work, or with publicizing the show. Parents should also be encouraged to attend the talent show performance.

The activity title *Talent Show* describes an activity that is a staple of family reunions, summer camps, workplaces, community groups, houses of worship, libraries, and schools. Talent shows allow participants to perform in a wide variety of fine arts media.

Procedure. Tell children if there is a talent show theme. At CISNT (Communities in Schools North Texas), the after-school program at Strickland Middle School where I volunteered as a chess teacher during spring 2010, most of the after-school children had just completed a three-week unit on the Olympic Games and were playing Wii games. My chess club had been playing chess. Therefore the CISNT talent show theme was initially planned to be "celebrating success and fun in games." In reality, the acts didn't follow this particular theme. Nevertheless, I required that my chess club children have a chess theme for their talent show submissions. Inform children that everyone may submit one artwork to the talent show. As long as the artwork is appropriate for the audience and shows effort, it will pass the audition stage.

Tell children that there will also be talent show auditions for dancers, musicians, and thespians. Display Figure 4.7. Point out to the children that the form favors group acts over soloists. For each child in a group, another point is added to the group's score. Short acts of three minutes or less also get more points than acts that last more than three minutes. Three reasons are behind my design of Figure 4.7. First, children must cooperate within groups. Second, by favoring groups, more children participate in the talent show. Third, time constraints favor short group performances over lengthy solo performances. To emphasize different factors, redesign Figure 4.7.

Between when children first encounter Figure 4.7 and the audition date, allow children to decide on and rehearse their acts. As budget and space permits, provide supplies. CISNT provided manila paper and crayons for artwork. Some children, however, preferred their own art supplies. During snack time, children in CISNT had cafeteria space and outdoor space to rehearse music, dance, and theater acts. Some children also rehearsed outside of after-school time and space.

Parents, relatives, and friends should be invited to the talent show performance. That talent show will include a display of the visual art and performances by the soloists or groups selected from the audition. If visual art winners are to be announced, display each artwork anonymously, with a number on its front. That is, children should write their names on the back of their visual art. Visiting parents, relatives, friends, and the child artists and performers fill out ballots listing their favorite, second-favorite, and third-favorite artwork. For example, a completed artwork ballot might read: 1st place: #4; 2nd place: #1; 3rd place: #9. If the live acts will be judged, the program listing the live acts can be used as a ballot. Include instructions for audience members and child artists and performers to write "1st place" next to their favorite act, "2nd place" next to their second-favorite act, and "3rd place" next to their third-favorite act.

At the CISNT Talent Show, no winners were selected and no ballots were used. Instead, after the show ended, every talent show participant picked a small prize from a pile of choices. Figure 4.8 shows eighth graders performing "Anthem" from the musical *Chess*. A YouTube video of their talent show performance is at http://www.youtube.com/watch?v=E_0VbtTs57A

Assessment. The teacher may formatively evaluate the rehearsal techniques of dancers, musicians, and thespians. The teacher may also provide formative feedback to the visual artists. On the audition day, children assess live acts with Figure 4.7. On the talent show day, children may complete ballots for favorite artwork and vote for favorite live acts. Likewise, the teacher fills out Figure 4.7. The teacher should be the sole judge on audition day of whether an artwork progresses to the talent show. The teacher collects completed copies of Figure 4.7. If winners for the talent show are to be selected, the teacher should tabulate the visual art ballots and the program votes for live acts.

Figure 4.8.
Talent show performance.

Chapter 5

CHESS BASICS

This chapter contains the rules of chess, algebraic notation, and Internet sites for practicing chess.

Rules of Chess

Starting position of a chess game

Queen on her own color

Figure 5.1.
Starting position of a chess game.

Let's Play Chess

Chess is a game for two players, one with the white chessmen and one with the black chessmen. The term "pieces" refers to the kings, queens, rooks, bishops, and knights only. Pawns are called pawns. At the beginning of the game, the chessmen are set up as shown in Figure 5.1. These hints will help you remember the proper board setup:

1. The white king and the black king are directly opposite each other.
2. The square in each player's lower right-hand corner is a light (white) one. Remember the expression "light on right."
3. The white queen goes on a light square, and the black queen on a dark square.

The Chessmen and How They Move

White always moves first, and then the players take turns moving. Only one piece or pawn may be moved at each turn (except for **castling,** as explained later in this chapter under the heading "Special Moves"). Chessmen

Black king on e5 can move to black Xs

White king on a3 can move to white Xs

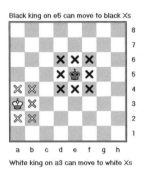

Figure 5.2.
Moves of the king (K).

move along unblocked lines. But the knight also may jump over other chessmen. You may not move a chessman to a square already occupied by your own pawn or piece. But you may capture an opponent's chessman that stands on a square where one of your chessmen can move. Simply remove the opponent's piece or pawn from the board and put your own chessman in its place (except for the en passant pawn capture, as explained in "Special Moves"). Although touching pieces and pawns may be helpful when solving chess problems, the **touch move** rule should apply in every chess game where **wins, losses,** and **draws** are recorded.

Generally speaking, the side with the stronger army will win. The strength of your army is determined by **points.** For example, trading a knight (worth three points) for a queen (worth nine points) is usually a good idea, because the trade leaves you the equivalent of six points ahead. The value of a pawn is one point, so a knight is worth three pawns or three points. A chessman's mobility determines its value, or points.

Black queen is on the square c6

Legal moves are marked with black Xs

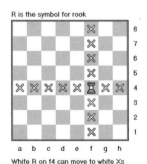

Figure 5.3.
Moves of the queen (Q).

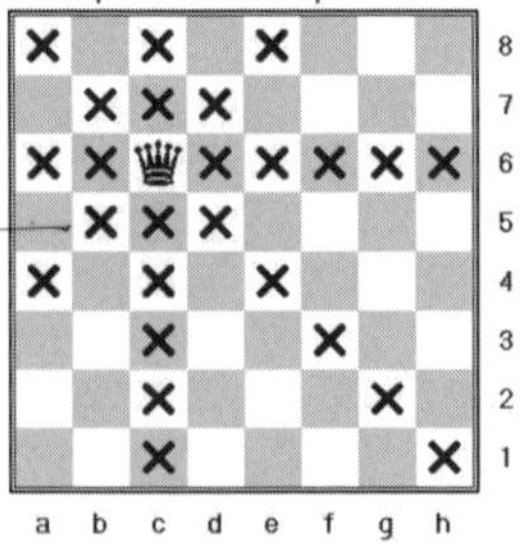

The King

The king has the symbol K. The graphic ♔ represents the white king, and ♚ is the black king. When the king is in **checkmate** his whole army loses. Therefore, in one sense, the king's point value is infinite. However, his actual value is generally about three points according to Wolff (2005, p. 76) and close to four points in the endgame according to USCF and Kurzdorfer (2003, p. 96). The king can move one square in any direction—for example, to any of the squares with Xs in Figure 5.2. The king may never move into check—that is, onto a square where it could be captured by an opponent's piece or pawn. If conditions are correct, the king may castle once per game (explained in "Special Moves").

The Queen

The queen is the most powerful piece and has the symbol Q. The graphic ♕ represents the white queen, and ♛ is the black queen. The queen is worth nine points. If her path is not blocked, the queen can move any number of squares horizontally, vertically, or diagonally. She can reach any of the squares with black Xs in Figure 5.3.

R is the symbol for rook

White R on f4 can move to white Xs

Figure 5.4.
Moves of the rook (R).

The Rook

The rook is the next most powerful piece and has the symbol R. The graphic ♖ represents the white rooks, and ♜ symbolizes the black rooks. The rook is worth five points. The rook can move any number of squares vertically or horizontally if its path is not blocked. The rook can reach any of the squares with white Xs in Figure 5.4.

Bishop on c8 can move to black Xs

Bishop on c1 can move to white Xs

Figure 5.5.
Moves of the bishop (B).

The Bishop

The bishop has the symbol B and has the graphic ♗ for white's bishops and ♝ for black's bishops. The bishop is generally considered to be worth three points, though some chess writers place the bishop's value slightly higher, for example, "3 points (plus a teensy bit more)" (Wolff, 2005, p. 75). The bishop can move any number of squares diagonally if its path is not blocked. At the beginning of the game, each side has one light-squared bishop and one dark-squared bishop. In Figure 5.5, the white bishop on c1 is white's dark- or black-squared bishop. It must stay on the black squares, marked by white Xs. In Figure 5.5, black's bishop on c8 is a light or white-squared bishop. It can move to the white squares marked by black Xs.

The Knight

The knight has the symbol N and has the graphic ♘ for white's knights and ♞ for black's knights. The knight is worth three points. The knight may hop over any chessmen in between its old and new squares. Think of the knight's move as the capital letter "L." It moves two squares horizontally, or two squares vertically, and then makes a right-angle turn onto its destination square. The knight always lands on a square opposite in color from its prior square. Figure 5.6 shows the N's moves with black Xs.

Knight on c4 can move to black Xs

Knight can jump over pieces and pawns

Figure 5.6.
Moves of the knight (N).

The Pawn

The pawn has the symbol P, but pawn moves are notated by stating the square the pawn moves to without use of the P. The graphic symbol for the white pawns is ♙, and the symbol for the black pawns is ♟. A pawn is worth one point (one pawn). The pawn moves straight ahead (never backward), but it captures diagonally. It moves one square at a time, but on its first move it has the option of moving forward either one or two squares.

In Figure 5.7, the circles indicate possible destinations for the pawns. The white pawn is on its original square, so it may move ahead either one or two squares. The black pawn has previously moved, so it may move ahead only one square at a time. The squares on which these pawns may make captures are indicated by Xs. However, captures would be possible only if enemy chessmen were on the X-ed squares.

If a pawn advances to the opposite end of the board, it is immediately promoted to a piece. It may not remain a pawn or become a king. A pawn may promote to a queen (or R, or N, or B) even if the original piece is on the board. If the original queen is on the board, one can use an upside-down rook to symbolize the just-promoted queen. In Figure 5.7, the promotion square for the white pawn is e8 and the promotion square for the black pawn is b1. The notation for promotion to a queen

Black pawn can move to b5

White pawn can move to e3 or e4

Figure 5.7.
Moves of the pawn (P).

Figure 5.8.
Before castling.

Figure 5.9.
After castling.

in the case of the white pawn would be e8(Q). The promotion of the black pawn to a rook would be notated b1(R).

Special Moves

There are two special moves in the game of chess. The first, castling, occurs in almost every chess game between experienced chess players. The second, en passant, is possible in less than 1 game out of 10 (USCF & Kurzdorfer, 2003, p. 62).

Castling

Each player may castle only once during a game, when certain conditions are met. Castling lets a player move two pieces at once: the king and one rook. Castling allows you to place your king in a safe location and also allows the castled rook to become more active. When the move is legal, each player has the choice of castling **kingside** or **queenside** or not at all, no matter what the other player chooses to do.

The procedure for castling is to move your king two squares toward the king's rook (kingside) or two squares toward the queen's rook (queenside). At the same time, the rook involved goes to the square beside the king and toward the middle of the board. Kingside castling is sometimes called "castling short" and queenside castling is "castling long" (Khmelnitsky, Khodarkovsky, & Zadorozny, 2006, Book 1, p. 89; King, 2000, p. 26). Figures 5.8 and 5.9 show castling.

In order to castle, neither the king nor the rook involved may have moved before. Also, the king may not castle out of check, into check, or through check. Furthermore, there may not be pieces of either color between the king and the rook involved in castling.

En Passant

En passant (e.p.) is a French phrase meaning "in passing." It is used to describe a special pawn capture. When one player moves a pawn two squares forward so that it is on an adjacent file and the same rank as an opponent's pawn, that opponent's pawn can capture the double-jumping pawn as if it had moved only one square. However, if the opponent's pawn does not exercise the en passant capture immediately, the option disappears for that particular e.p. capture. But new opportunities may arise for pawns in similar circumstances.

The rule originated when pawns gained the double-jump power on their first move, which occurred shortly after the 1450s (King, 2000, pp. 8, 27). To keep some consistency despite the rule change, the en passant rule arose so that one could capture the double-jumping pawn as if it had moved only one square. Figure 5.10 shows black's choices. If black takes en passant (1 . . . . dxc3 e.p.), black's pawn ends up on c3 and the white pawn on c4 is removed from the board.

Figure 5.10.
The en passant (e.p.) rule.

About Check, Checkmate, and Stalemate

The ultimate goal of chess is to checkmate your opponent's king. The king is not actually captured and removed from the board. But if the king is checked, it must get out of check immediately. If there is no way to get out of check, then the position is a checkmate. The side that is checkmated loses.

You may not move into check. For example, moving into a direct line with your opponent's rook if there are no chessmen between that rook and your king is an **illegal** move. The rook could capture your king, which is not allowed.

If you are put into check by your opponent's move, there are three ways of getting out of check:

1. Capture the checking piece or pawn;
2. Place one of your own chessmen between the checking chessman and your king. Blockading doesn't work against a knight or a pawn;
3. Move your king away from the check.

If a checked player has none of these three escapes, then that player is checkmated and loses the game. In a chess tournament, a checkmate is scored as a win (one point) for the player delivering the checkmate.

In contrast, if a player is not in check but has no legal move, the position is called a **stalemate.** A stalemate is scored as a draw, or tie (half a point), for each player.

These preceding rules of chess were adapted from *Let's Play Chess* (USCF, 1998), a brochure formerly available from the United States Chess Federation. The next two sections of chapter 5—"Win, Lose, or Draw" and "Reading and Writing Chess"—illustrate what happens when chess games are under way.

Win, Lose, or Draw

As noted in the rules of chess, checkmate or stalemate ends a chess game. A check, however, is temporary. When the king escapes from check, the game continues. Figure 5.11 has exercises to identify check, checkmate, and stalemate. The answer key for Figure 5.11 is in Appendix A. Stalemate is just one of several ways that chess games can be drawn; see *draws* in the glossary.

Reading and Writing Chess

Playing chess games is one way to improve at chess; learning chess notation is another improvement method. Reading notation enables you to study games in newspaper chess columns, in chess magazines, and in chess books. Notating your chess games allows review of those games later with a friend, parent, teacher, or chess coach.

For each diagram, tell whether the position is a check, a mate (checkmate), or a stalemate. Write your answer in the space below the diagram.

Black to move. Check, mate, or stalemate

Diagram 1

_____

Black to move. Check, mate, or stalemate

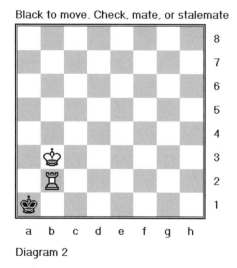

Diagram 2

_____

White to move. Check, mate, or stalemate

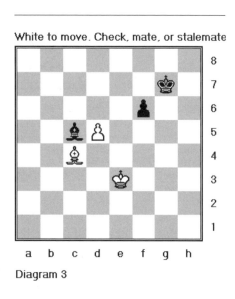

Diagram 3

_____

White to move. Check, mate, or stalemate

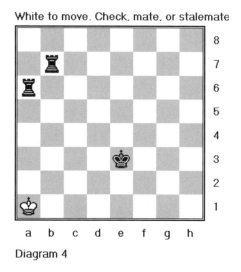

Diagram 4

_____

Figure 5.11
Check, Checkmate, or Stalemate?

From *The Living Chess Game: Fine Arts Activities for Kids 9–14* by Alexey W. Root. Santa Barbara, CA: Libraries Unlimited. Copyright © 2011.

Figure 5.12.

Figure 5.13.

Figure 5.14.

To practice algebraic chess notation, I present the first seven moves of the Evans **gambit**. The Evans gambit was a popular chess **opening** in the 1800s and is characterized by white's 4. b4. That move sacrifices the b-pawn to speed up **development** and control of the **center**. The moves are from the Evergreen game in Appendix C.

1. e4 e5 2. Nf3 Nc6 3. Bc4 Bc5 4. b4 Bxb4 5. c3 Ba5 6. d4 exd4 7. 0-0 d3 Now I will explain how each move was notated.

1. e4 Figure 5.12 shows the move 1. e4 on the board. The white pawn that sits in front of the white king moved two squares forward. The square is named e4, derived from the file-name (e) and the rank name (4). When a pawn (P) moves there, we could write Pe4, but it is traditional not to list the P when notating pawn moves. **1. . . . e5** The ellipsis points (. . .) before the move let us know that the pawn move e5 was a move for black. Figure 5.13 shows the position after black moved the pawn in front of black's king two squares forward. **2. Nf3** The position after white's second move is shown in Figure 5.14. The capital letter N stands for knight, since K is used as an abbreviation for king. **2. . . . Nc6** Black replied with a knight's move from b8 to c6. The resulting position is shown in Figure 5.15. **3. Bc4** The B stands for bishop. The resulting position is shown in Figure 5.16. Now follow the next several moves on your set and board. **3. . . . Bc5 4. b4 Bxb4** An "x" means capture in notation; therefore, this move was the black bishop capturing the b-pawn. **5. c3 Ba5 6. d4 exd4 7. 0-0** This notation means kingside castling. You can use zeroes or capital letter Os for castling. Queenside castling is written 0-0-0. Other special symbols are +, written at the end of a move to show that the move gave a check; # or + + designates giving checkmate. **7. . . . d3**. The position after black's seventh move is shown in Figure 5.17. Does the position in Figure 5.17 match what you played out on your board? If so, good job!

Figure 5.15.

Figure 5.16.

Figure 5.17.

Internet Sites for Practicing Chess

Dalby (2003, p. 6) advises youngsters to be safe on the Internet. In general, her guidelines for safe visits to chess Web sites are the same as for visiting any Web site. Ask for parent or guardian permission before connecting to the Internet. Never give out your full name, address, or telephone number. Before registering at a Web site, ask an adult for permission. Never respond to an e-mail from someone you do not know. Do not meet in person with someone that you know only from the Internet.

Nowadays, you can play chess at many general-purpose Web sites such as Yahoo! Some of the more popular chess-specific Web sites are the Internet Chess Club, http://www.chessclub.com/; the Free Internet Chess Server, http://www.freechess.org/; Playchess.com, http://play chess.com/; and Chess.com, http://www.chess.com/. The live chess games and instructional lectures on these sites appeal mostly to teens and adults.

In the remainder of this chapter I describe Web sites designed for chess beginners and intermediates ages 9–14. The sites I highlight teach the rules of chess but also progress to tactics, basic checkmates, and openings. They provide free content. Some feature chess games against a computer:

- http://www.chesskids.com/ is the most comprehensive site, with free online chess lessons and a chance to play against a computer. The lessons use simple language and engaging cartoon graphics. The site also has chess resources for teachers and parents.
- http://www.chesskid.com/ is a rapidly growing site with new instructional articles and videos added every week, live chess with other humans and the computer, safety features, and a large database of tactics problems.
- http://www.chessdryad.com/education/magictheater/index.htm is a collection of Flash movies showing the rules of chess, tactics, and checkmating patterns.
- http://www.chesscorner.com/ has graphics and text that appeal to children 12 and older or adults. It covers the rules of chess and has games and quotes from famous chess players.
- http://www.kidchess.com/ has colorful photos and graphics. It also features chess problems and a chance to play against computer opponents of different levels.
- http://www.50chessgames.freeserve.co.uk/ gives examples of chess games played by chess beginners. Every move is analyzed and displayed with a detailed commentary written for beginners.
- http://www.educationalchess.com/ has chess rules, chess hangman, chess crosswords, and a gallery of chess-themed art.

I write articles for http://www.chesskid.com/. The creator of http://www.educationalchess.com/ is a friend of mine. Other than those connections, I have no personal or business relationships with the listed chess sites for ages 9–14. Some of the sites I picked are among the dozens of links in Dalby (2003). I checked URLs in September of 2010. Nevertheless, links change over time. A good place to check for current links is the United States Chess Federation, http://www.uschess.org.

Appendix A

ANSWER KEY

The Answer Key gives the parent information and release forms referred to in chapter 1. The Answer Key also provides examples of children's work from some of the 12 activities in chapters 2–4. It also gives the answers for Figure 5.11. The answers for chapters 2–4 are illustrative rather than definitive. That is, one knight song will differ from another. Scripts vary, even if based on the same famous game or problem. In the arts, multiple outcomes are encouraged and expected. As Gelineau (2004) wrote:

> The educational value of the arts lies in the process—not the product; thus, the intent is not to train artists; rather, it is to affirm the power of the arts as a learning tool and a vital force in human existence. (p. 17)

Chapter 1

Figure A.1 is the information sent to parents at the start of the August 3–7, 2009, MOSAIC camp. Figure A.2 is the release form for parents to sign for their children's work and photo to appear in this book.

Figure A.3 is the press release for the Denton Public Library chess classes, modified to show the change of performance date from Saturday, November 21, to Tuesday, November 24, at 4 P.M.

Figure A.4 is the calendar for the Denton Public Library (North Branch) for November 2009. There was a similar calendar for October 2009 not reproduced here.

PARENT INFORMATION LETTER.

To: Parents of chess class students

Early morning class is 9 to 10:30 A.M.

Late morning class is 10:30 to noon

August 3–7, 2009

Please send chess students with:

1) notebook paper or blank paper

2) pen or pencil

3) folder

4) Optional: If you have an artistic chess set and board to display for our chess class, please send that along too.

For our living chess game on Friday, half the students will be asked to wear a white or light-colored shirt. The other half will be asked to wear a black (or dark-colored) shirt.

Please plan to attend the living chess game performance during the second half of your child's class on Friday. The second halves are: 9:45 to 10:30 for the early morning group, and 11:15 to noon for the late-morning group.

If you wish to also participate in the simultaneous chess exhibition (a "simul," where all students play individually or with parent help against the teacher), show up for the ENTIRE class on Friday. On Friday, we will have the simul during the first half of class, and the performance during the second half of class.

Also, please consider printing out and signing the attached form so that I can feature your child's work and/or photo in my upcoming (2011) book The Living Chess Game: Fine Arts Activities for Kids Ages 9–14.

Our schedule for the week, mostly in room B109:

Monday: Music and chess; ladder game 1. In a ladder game, each student challenges another student. If you win, you move higher on the ladder.

Tuesday: Dance and chess; ladder game 2

Wednesday: Art and chess; ladder game 3

Thursday: Theater and chess; ladder game 4; rehearsals in cafeteria for Living Chess Game

Friday: First half of class in B109 for the simul; second half of class in cafeteria for performance of the Living Chess Game.

On each day, I will also be teaching chess rules, chess strategies, and we will study famous chess games and positions. Students will be performing a famous chess game or chess position as a Living Chess Game on Friday.

Thank you,

Dr. Alexey Root (MOSAIC chess instructor)

Figure A.1.
Parent information letter.

MODEL AND STUDENT WORK RELEASE FORM.

STUDENT WORK AND PHOTO RELEASE FORM

The parent or guardian _____ of the student _____ grants to the author/photographer Dr. Alexey Root and to her assignees and licensees the absolute right and permission to use, publish, or sell the student work(s) and the photograph(s) created during MOSAIC Chess Camp (August 3–7, 2009), in which the student has created work or is included in photos, in any medium, throughout the world, without any restriction whatsoever as to the nature of the use or publication or as to the copy of any printed matter accompanying the photograph(s). I understand that the student work and the images may be altered and I waive the right to approve of any finished product. I understand that I do not own the copyright of the student work or the photograph(s). I certify that I am over 18 years of age and that I have the full legal right to execute this agreement.

NAME of author/photographer: Alexey Root

DESCRIPTION of student work: Students' written assignments about different aspects of chess. The student certifies that the work is original. Students will be identified by first name and age only.

DESCRIPTION of photography: Photos of students playing chess or working on chess camp assignments. Student will be identified by first name and age only.

SIGNATURE of student: DATE:

NAME of student:

AGE of student (if under 18 years of age):

Name of Parent/Guardian

Signature of Parent/Guardian

ADDRESS of student:

_____

_____

Telephone: _____

Email address: _____

Figure A.2.
Model and student work release form

August 11, 2009   John Cabrales Jr.
FOR IMMEDIATE RELEASE   Public Information Officer
                                             940-349-8509 office
                                             940-380-3520 pager
                                             940-465-4846 mobile
                                             E-mail: john.cabrales@cityofdenton.com

Living Chess Game at the Library

Denton, TX –

Children can learn the rules of chess by participating in a living chess game to be staged at the North Branch Library. This unique twelve-week program for 9 to 14 year olds will transform participants into singing, dancing chessmen! Dr. Alexey Root, author of *Children and Chess: A Guide for Educators* and former U.S. Women's chess champion, will direct the program.

The *Living Chess* group will meet on Thursdays at 2:30 p.m. beginning September 3. The program will culminate with a performance on November 24 at 4 p.m. This class is free and open to the public. Space is limited and registration is required.

For more information, contact WyLaina Hildreth, Public Services Librarian, at 940.349.8774 or at wylaina.hildreth@cityofdenton.com

For other news items on the City of Denton, visit our website at www.cityofdenton.com, go to Quick Information, and click on Press Releases.

####

Figure A.3.
Press release.

From *The Living Chess Game: Fine Arts Activities for Kids 9–14* by Alexey W. Root. Santa Barbara, CA: Libraries Unlimited. Copyright © 2011.

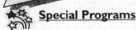

North Branch Library
November 2009

Special Programs

Living Chess - Thursdays at 2:30 pm
Children can learn the rules of chess by participating in a living chess game at the North Branch Library. This 12 week program for 9 to 14 year olds will transform participants into singing, dancing chessmen! Dr. Alexey Root, author of *Children and Chess: A Guide for Educators* and former U.S. Women's chess champion, will direct the program. Call 940.349.8744 to register or email Wylaina Hildreth at wylaina.hildreth@cityofdenton.com

11/7 Denton Reads Book Discussion: Wicked - Saturday at 11 an
Come Discuss the book Wicked as we get ready for author Gregory Maguire to visit Denton.

11/10 Teen Advisory Board (TAB) - Tuesday at 6:30 pm
Join the Denton Public Library TAB to plan programs & projects for teens. We discuss books, films & music teens would like added to the library. Contact Juli Gonzalez at 349.8741 for more information.

11/13 Coupon Exchange - Friday at 10 am
Cut the high cost of groceries with coupons. Join your friends and neighbors on the second Friday of the month at the North Branch Library.

11/14 Writing Workshop - Saturday at 2 pm
If writing appeals to you either as a hobby or professionally come to our monthly writing workshops at the North Branch Library every 2nd Saturday of the month. Workshops will cover various aspects of writing. Feel free to attend any or all of the workshops.

11/24 Living Chess Game - Tuesday at 4 pm
The students from Living Chess play a game using themselves as pieces!

Denton Reads

Presents

Gregory Maguire

November 21, 2009
6:00 pm
Texas Woman's University

Turn page over for calendar view.

Weekly Programs

Mother Goose - Fridays at 10am
25-30 minutes of stories and activities for infants, birth through 18 months, and their caregivers.

StoryTime - Fridays at 11am
25-30 minutes of stories, songs, puppets, and more for children ages 1-5 and their caregivers.

Book Adventures - Tuesdays at 4pm
40-45 minutes of books, crafts, and activities for children in kindergarten through 3rd grade.

Bilingual StoryTime - Saturdays at 10am
Stories for children in both English and Spanish.
Cuentos para los niños en inglés y español.

Basic Mandarin Chinese for Kids - Fridays at 5pm
Learn Chinese characters from Jia-Jia Zhang. She's only 9 yrs old, but she knows how to make learning Mandarin fun! Call 349-8752 to register. Grades K-5.

Teen CLIC - Tuesdays at 4pm
Come hang out in our computer lab with friends. Every Tuesday, 4 -5 pm on school days. This program is for teens in grades 6 -12.

Teen Game Day - Wednesdays at 4pm
Come play Guitar Hero, Dance Dance Revolution, Play Station 2 games or the Wii every Wednesday at the North Branch Library from 4-5 on school days. This program is best for teens in grades 6-12.

Clubs and Groups

Chess Night –Mondays from 6-9 pm
Adults and children learn chess and play in tournaments.

Animanga - Third Wednesday of the month at 6:30 pm
Watch, read and draw all things anime. Snacks provided.
For teens in 6-12th grade.

North Branch Writers' Critique group - Tuesdays at 7pm
Whether you like writing novels, short stories, poetry or journals you should come check out the *North Branch Writers' Critique Group*. For more information or to register, call Annie Neugerbauer at 979-220-3666 or email annie_07@alumni.utexas.net

Adult Graphic Novel Book Club - Wednesday at 7 pm
Read and discuss great graphic novels. For information contact WyLaina at 349-8774. November discussion: Any book in the *Kurosagi Corpse Delivery Service* series by Eiji Ohtshuka.

Philosophy for Fun - 11/3 &11/17 at 7 pm.
Come & chat about philosophical questions of your choosing with Dr. Eva H. Cadwallader, professor of philosophy, emerita. Call 349.8752 to register.

Small Talk Conversation Group -
Wednesdays 7 pm & Saturdays at 12:30 pm
A program to practice English for those of different cultures in a relax environment. This is **not** a program to learn English, only a way to improve English speaking skills. Space is limited. Call 940.349.8752 to register.

Figure A.4.
Denton Public Library (North Branch) Calendar.

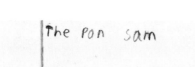

Figure A.5.
Notes and lyrics by a 12-year-old.

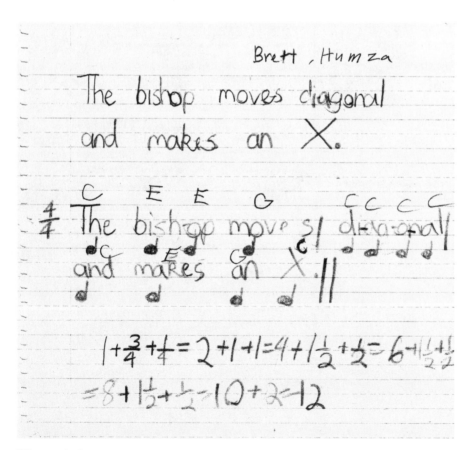

Figure A.6.
Chapter 2 assignments.

Figure A.7.
Composing at the keyboard..

Chapter 2

For *Activity One,* 9-year-old Kaila and 10-year-old Bilal wrote these two lines about the king:

The king moves one space
in every direction.

For *Activity Two,* the answers for Figure 2.3 are 1. 4/4 2. quarter note 3. four beats 4. half note. 5. end of the measure 6. end of the piece [It's not really the end of the entire "Twinkle, Twinkle" song, but it is the end of the excerpt for our purposes.] 7. yes 8. twin-kle.

Twelve-year-old Sam wrote the lyrics and notes about the pawn shown in Figure A.5.

Figure A.6 has assignments from all three activities in chapter 2. Included are the two lines of lyrics (from *Activity One*), the syllables and note values (from *Activity Two*), and the treble-clef notes (from *Activity Three*) composed by two boys, ages eight and nine. Also included in Figure A.6, from *Activity Three*, are the note values of each measure in Figure 2.7. A photo of the two boys working at the keyboard is in Figure A.7.

For *Activity Three,* 10-year-old Ashleigh composed music and lyrics about the knight. A library staff person and a parent volunteer transcribed the musical notation for Ashleigh. Figure A.8 is a handwritten copy of their in-class work.

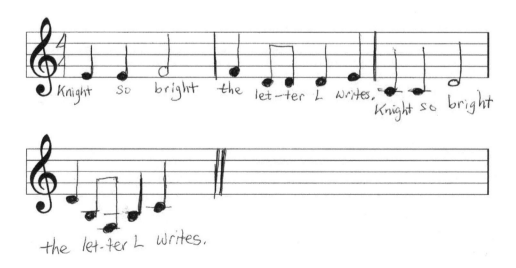

Figure A.8.
Musical notation and lyrics by a 10-year-old.

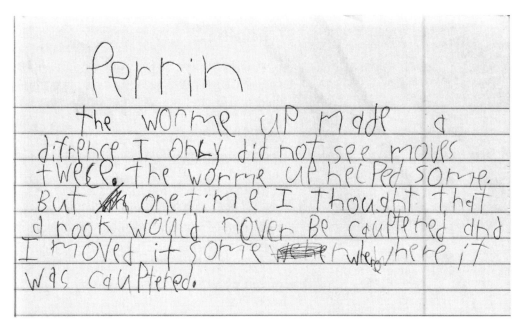

Figure A.9.
Effect of warm-up on chess game.

Chapter 3

For *Activity Five,* eight-year-old Perrin participated in the warm-up and then played a chess game. Then he wrote about the effects of the warm-up. For example, thanks to the warm-up, Perrin wrote that he anticipated his opponent's moves on all but two of those moves. His sentences are in Figure A.9.

For *Activity Six,* 10-year-old Alexandra thought the chessmen in Figure 3.3 were wood and rock. They are actually plastic. I have corrected Alexandra's spelling but otherwise quoted her answers to Figure 3.2.

Description: Culture China, finely carved, wood & (rock), red & black squares, slightly out of shape. Metal hinges. Metal handle. Analysis: Texture: bumpy/rough, somewhat smooth. Value: deep. Color: brown/black & yellow/tan. Size: King, queen & bishop tallest. Pretty/Golden Dragon. Interpretation: It says chess is regal, elegant, hard, fun, deft, & powerful. Says king and queen are more important. Judgment: It is very beautiful. I love it. I would totally buy it! I would display it & play with it. It is very admirable.

For *Activity Seven,* nine-year-old Anabelle drew the publicity poster for the Super Mario–themed living chess game performance at the

Figure A.10.
Super Mario living chess game poster.

Move, i.e., 1. e4 or 1. . . . e5	What white felt or thought Optional: Include facial expression such as L ☹	What black felt or thought Optional: Include facial expression such as ☺
4. Kd6	My pawn is cornered.	No!
4. . . . h2	Shoot!	My queen is coming.
5. c7	Mine too!	No!
6. . . . h1(Q)	Oh shoot!	I rock!
7. c8 (Q)	I have my queen.	No!

Figure A.11.
A 10-year-old's answers for Figure 4.1.

Denton Public Library. Anabelle is on the right side of Figure A.10. Also pictured, on the left in Figure A.10, is nine-year-old Deborah. Both Anabelle and Deborah regularly attended my Living Chess Game classes.

Chapter 4

For *Activity Eight,* 10-year-old Alex annotated the Réti endgame from Appendix C in Figure A.11. Spellings have been corrected from Alex's original, and I have typed his handwritten words. A script from children who attended the 2009 MOSAIC 10:30–noon class is in Figure A.12. That script refers to costuming based on *The Simpsons* (animated TV series) chess set shown in Williams (2000, pp. 154–155).

Chapter 5

For Figure 5.11, Diagram 1 is a checkmate, Diagram 2 is a stalemate, Diagram 3 is a check, and Diagram 4 is a checkmate.

SIMPSONS-THEMED CHESS SCRIPT

10:30 to noon class, August 3–7, 2009, MOSAIC

Preshow: Chris O., Mason, and Riley perform chess-move music and dance-move captures.

Main show: Réti endgame, with Simpsons-themed chessmen.

Character name	Actor
NARRATOR ONE	Trey
NARRATOR TWO	Chris O.
NARRATOR THREE	Chris S.
NARRATOR FOUR	Philip
NARRATOR FIVE	Jake
NARRATOR SIX	Riley
NARRATOR SEVEN	Tanya
WHITE KING	Bilal
BLACK KING	Kaila
WHITE PAWN	Brett
BLACK PAWN	Mason
WHITE QUEEN	Emma
BLACK QUEEN	Alex (Alexandra)

This is a one-act play with no intermission. Starting position, with white to play and draw, is shown in Figure C.41: White: Kh8, pawn on c6. Black: Ka6, pawn on h5. Solution: **1. Kg7 h4 2. Kf6 Kb6 3. Ke5 h3 4. Kd6 h2 5. c7 Kb7 6. Kd7 h1(Q) 7. c8(Q)+ 1/2–1/2.**

The play begins with all the actors (living chessmen and narrators) next to the chessboard stage, facing the audience. The chessmen are seated on the floor, and the narrators are standing.

The following stage directions apply during the play, but are printed here so as not to confuse the narrators about their lines. As each piece and pawn is introduced, he or she moves onto the chessboard (walking like a character from the Simpsons) to the correct starting square listed for the Réti problem. The queens move just offside of the board: The white queen moves to a space next to the square c8, and the black queen moves to a space next to the square h1.

Movement songs: The kings sing "The king moves one square in any direction." The pawns sing, "Pawns move forward one." Each queen improvises when her side's pawn promotes. The black queen will dance, and the white queen will dance and say check. The promoted pawns wait by the side of the board for the final bow.

NARRATOR ONE: Richard Réti was one of the top players in the world in the 1910s and 1920s. He lived in Prague, in what is now Slovakia. In 1925, he played 29 games blindfolded, winning 21 and drawing six. He died at the age of 40, of scarlet fever. In 1921 Réti published this endgame problem.

NARRATOR TWO: The white king is played by Bilal. The black king is played by Kaila. The white pawn is played by Brett. The black pawn is played by Mason. The white queen is played by Emma. The black queen is played by Alex.

NARRATOR THREE: This is the 21st century so we decided that we would use a more modern model. We chose the symbol of comedy, *The Simpsons!*

NARRATOR FOUR: The white king moves to g7. The black pawn moves to h4. The white king moves to f6. The black king moves to b6. The white pawn is in danger. The horror!

The faces of the white chessmen show dismay.

NARRATOR FIVE: The white king moves to e5. The white king has a threat of moving to f4, catching up with the black h-pawn. The black pawn moves to h3.

NARRATOR SIX: The white king moves to d6. The black pawn moves to h2. The white pawn moves to c7. The black king moves to b7.

NARRATOR SEVEN: The white king moves to d7. The black pawn moves to h1, and is promoted to a queen. The white pawn moves to c8, and is promoted to a queen.

ALL NARRATORS: And the game was drawn.

At this point the chessmen leave the chessboard stage to join the narrators in a line in front of the chessboard stage. All the actors take a bow together.

Figure A.12.
Simpsons-themed chess script.

From *The Living Chess Game: Fine Arts Activities for Kids 9–14* by Alexey W. Root. Santa Barbara, CA: Libraries Unlimited. Copyright © 2011.

Appendix B

REFERENCES

References (Annotated)

ArtsAlive.ca (2009). Retrieved July 11, 2009 from http://www.artsalive.ca/en/ My chapter 1 quote about actors doubling in roles is from the essay "Putting on a play: step-by-step" retrieved from http://www.artsalive.ca/en/thf/faire/creation.html. The citation in chapter 3, *Activity Seven,* is to the essay "Design and Production" retrieved from http://www.artsalive.ca/en/eth/design/. That essay has information and activities about design and production, including set and costume design.

Barron, R. (n.d.). Systems of the body: Movement and choreography. *ARTSEDGE.* Retrieved from http://artsedge.kennedy-center.org/content/2012/ Barron's five lesson plans teach students in grades 5–8 to create movement patterns that express information about the human body. I borrowed the elements of "complementary actions" and that "each performance must have a beginning, a middle, and an end."

Bever, L. (2009, November 3). Hedrick Elementary students become real-life chess pieces. *neighborsgo.* Retrieved from http://neighborsgo.com/stories/45450 This article tells how The Village Church donated an outdoor chessboard to Hedrick Elementary School in Lewisville, Texas. Then Billy Kyer, a Flower Mound High School student, raised more than $1,100 to build four picnic tables, four benches, and make costumes (shirts). Each shirt had a graphic of a particular chessman and that chessman's name in English and Spanish.

Bronson, P., & Merryman, A. (2009). *Nurtureshock: New thinking about children.* New York: Twelve. Journalists compile and explain recent findings in child development, such as the inverse power of praise on motivation.

Cheng, T. L. (2009, August 1). Up close and personal with prof Kenneth Rogoff. *The Star Online.* Retrieved from http://biz.thestar.com.my/news/story.asp?file=/2009/8/1/business/4401017&sec=business The Star Online is the Internet edition of Malaysia's leading English-language newspaper. Rogoff was interviewed at an economics seminar in Kuala Lumpur, Malaysia.

Chernev, I. (1955). *1000 best short games of chess.* New York: Simon & Schuster. This book contains games of 24 moves or less. Chernev includes annotations for the Immortal, Evergreen, and Opera games.

Dalby, E. (2003). *The Usborne internet-linked complete book of chess.* Tulsa, OK: EDC. This book is an introduction to the rules of chess, common openings, tactics, endgames, chess history, and chess champions. It includes Internet links to instructional chess Web sites.

Eade, J. (2005). *Chess for dummies* (2nd ed.). New York: Hungry Minds. This book covers the rules of chess, chess history, strategies and tactics, famous games, and tips for tournament and Internet chess play. Eade includes annotations, and biographical information about the players, for the Immortal, Evergreen, and Opera games.

Fine, R. (1941). *Basic chess endings.* New York: David McKay. This book is a comprehensive overview of the endgame for intermediate players and higher.

Fitch, G. (2006). The imagery of chess revisited at the Noguchi museum. *Artezine—A Cyberspace Review of the Arts, 13.* Retrieved from http://www.artezine.com/issues/20060701/imochess.html Fitch provides photos along the left margin of his article. Click on each photo to enlarge. Also provided is a history of the exhibition, a list of artists, and descriptions of their work. See List (2005) for expanded coverage of the Noguchi exhibition.

Gelineau, R. P. (2004). *Integrating the arts across the elementary school curriculum.* Belmont, CA: Wadsworth/Thomson Learning. The first two chapters tell why the arts are important in education. Later chapters on art, music, drama, and dance each contain several activities. This book is for educators of grades K–6.

Haley, C. (2008). Performance evaluation rubric. *Camille Thompson's Teaching Portfolio.* Retrieved from http://emerson.digication.com/camillethompson/Instruction/ and then click on the Performance Rubric.doc. This rubric provides guidance in evaluating students' acting.

Keres, P. (1974). *Practical chess endings.* (J. Littlewood, Trans.). New York: RHM. (Original work published 1973). Keres usually has more thorough annotations than Fine, but Fine has a greater variety of endgames. Keres annotates the Réti endgame. This RHM edition uses

descriptive notation. RHM published an algebraic notation edition in 1976.

Khmelnitsky, I., Khodarkovsky, M., & Zadorozny, M. (2006). *Teaching chess step by step.* Montville, NJ: Kasparov Chess Foundation. Schools may order a complimentary set of three books (1-Teacher's Manual, 2-Exercises Manual, and 3-Activities) by following the instructions at http://www.kasparovchessfoundation.org/.

King, D. (2000). *Chess: From first moves to checkmate.* Boston: Kingfisher. This book features striking artwork and many chess diagrams. King teaches the history and the rules of chess.

List, L. (Ed.). (2005). *The imagery of chess revisited.* New York: George Braziller. This catalog is for an Isamu Noguchi Garden Museum exhibition of artistic chess sets and boards from the early- to mid-20th century. The exhibition reprised the original exhibition of many of those sets and boards in 1944–1945. Referencing the elements of art and design, List critiques the sets and boards. Many color photographs are included. List and other contributors provide biographical information about the artists and explain historical connections.

McDonald, N. L., & Fisher, D. (2006). *Teaching literacy through the arts.* New York: Guilford. This book includes several projects that incorporate the arts when teaching language arts subjects such as haiku. The book also shows how to incorporate literacy when appreciating fine arts classics such as Smetana's *The Moldau.*

Mehlhaff, R. (2009, November 19). Pawns in their own chess game. *Denton Record-Chronicle,* p. 3 (Denton Time section). This article describes the living chess game classes at the Denton Public Library.

Meyer, R. G. (2002). *Articulation: Learning to look at art.* Retrieved from http://articulation.kcjenkins.com/ This Web site teaches art critiquing. Checklists for analysis, and artworks to critique, are provided.

Music Educators National Conference (MENC). (1994). *National standards for arts education: What every young American should know and be able to do in the arts.* Reston, VA: Author. Used by permission. The complete National Arts Standards and additional materials relating to the Standards are available from MENC: The National Association for Music Education, 1806 Robert Fulton Drive, Reston, VA 20191; http://www.menc.org.

Naumann, F. M., Bailey, B., & Shahade, J. (2009). *Marcel Duchamp: The art of chess.* New York: Readymade. This book explores how chess affected Duchamp's art. Jennifer Shahade, a two-time U.S. Women's Chess Champion, annotates 15 of Duchamp's chess games.

Note value. (2009, June 25). In *Wikipedia, The Free Encyclopedia.* Retrieved 12:21, June 25, 2009, from http://en.wikipedia.org/w/index.php?title=Note_value&oldid=298547744 I modified the note value chart. Chart is available for use under the Creative Commons license http://creativecommons.org/licenses/by-sa/3.0/.

Pandolfini, B. (1995). *Chess thinking.* New York: Fireside. This book is a dictionary of chess terms.

Rice, T. (lyrics), Andersson, B. (music), & Ulvaeus, B. (music). (2009). *Chess in concert* [DVD or CD]. United States: Warner Brothers. The musical *Chess* has been popular since its debut in the mid-1980s. Lyrics are by Tim Rice (*Jesus Christ Superstar, The Lion King, Evita*) and music by ABBA's Björn Ulvaeus and Benny Andersson. In 2008, a concert version was staged with Josh Groban and the London Philharmonic. A CD and DVD followed in 2009. The director of *Chess in Concert* was Hugh Wooldridge.

Root, A. W. (2006). *Children and chess: A guide for educators.* Westport, CT: Teacher Ideas Press. Early chapters give curricular reasons for educators to include chess. The latter part of the book has lesson plans, worksheets, and connections to state standards.

Root, A. W. (2008). *Science, math, checkmate: 32 chess activities for inquiry and problem solving.* Westport, CT: Teacher Ideas Press. Thirty-two plans organized by chess level and grade level (either 3–5 or 6–8) that teach science, math, or interdisciplinary objectives using chess.

Root, A. W. (2009). *Read, write, checkmate: Enrich literacy with chess activities.* Westport, CT: Teacher Ideas Press. This book explains the rules of chess and includes exercises. One of the instructional chapters was written by middle school students.

Royston, P. (2006). *The study guide for the* phantom of the opera. Retrieved from http://www.thephantomoftheopera.com/the_show/education.php This free study guide explains how various fine artists transformed *The Phantom of the Opera* novel (1911) into screenplays, musical theater, and movies. It includes research and discussion questions. It is available as a downloadable PDF file.

Schafroth, C. (2002). *The art of chess.* New York: Harry N. Abrams. Schafroth shows the connection between history and the materials and designs of chess sets. The book includes many photographs of chess sets and boards.

Shahade, J. (2009, March 6). Chess and art in Iceland. *Chess Life Online.* Retrieved from http://main.uschess.org/content/view/9180/520 Shahade posts photos and describes a 2009 exhibition of chess sets and boards at the Reykjavik Art Museum.

Shenk, D. (2006). *The immortal game: A history of chess, or how 32 carved pieces on a board illuminated our understanding of war, art, science, and the human brain.* New York: Doubleday. This popular nonfiction title highlights the origins of chess and famous people who played chess, and it ends with how chess is being taught in present-day inner city classrooms. Shenk includes annotations for every move, and a description of the players and the setting, of the Immortal game.

Sikes, M. (2007). *Building parent involvement through the arts: Activities and projects that enrich classrooms and schools.* Thousand Oaks, CA: Corwin Press. Sikes begins with the importance of arts to schools. His particular focus is on how the arts increase parent involvement. Sikes has chapters on visual arts, theater, dance, music, literary arts, and folk and traditional arts. Sikes includes reproducibles. What I call activities he calls projects. Most of his projects are for students in "various" or "multiple" grade levels, but he also has some projects for specified ranges (grades 1–8, grades 2–12, grades 4–12, and so forth).

Stefurak, L. (2004). Ask Dr. Leo—February 2004. *Northwest Chess.* Retrieved from http://www.nwchess.com/scholastic/dr_leo_200402. htm Stefurak explains appropriate pretournament and tournament day preparations for scholastic chess players. In chapter 3, *Activity Five,* I quoted a warm-up from about half-way down on the Web page http://www.nwchess.com/scholastic/dr_leo_200402.htm

Stevenson, S. E. (n.d.). Elements of dance. *ARTSEDGE.* Retrieved from http://artsedge.kennedy-center.org/content/2338/ This three-lesson unit teaches students in grades 5–8 the elements of movement. It includes a physical warm-up, in the Guided Practice section, which I quoted in chapter 3, *Activity Five.*

Stratakis, M. (1994). Find mate in 13 moves! *Manolis Stratakis Chess Problems Page.* Retrieved from http://www2.forthnet.gr/chess/ma tein13.html This same problem appears in a PDF of a Russian chess magazine, http://64.ru/files/64-2008-04-kogda-figuri.pdf, which attributes the problem to *American Chess Weekly,* 1909.

Thomas, L. (n.d.). Music composition. *ARTSEDGE.* Retrieved from http://artsedge.kennedy-center.org/content/2447/ This nine-week unit is for teaching music composition to students in grades 5–8. It has lesson plans and assessment for educators, and checklists for students. My first three activities cite several ideas (such as separating words into syllables and composing melodies) that are also covered by Thomas.

United States Chess Federation. (1998). *Let's play chess: Summary of the moves of chess.* Copy in possession of Alexey Root. This brochure was formerly available from the United States Chess Federation.

United States Chess Federation (USCF) & Kurzdorfer, P. (2003). *The everything chess basics book.* Avon, MA: Adams Media. This book is a comprehensive introduction to the game of chess, similar to Eade (2005).

Williams, G. (2000). *Master pieces: The story of chess: The pieces, players, and passion of 1,000 years.* London: Apple. This book has very few photographs of chess boards, but many photos of chessmen throughout history. The author also explains the history behind the forms, for example, why Islamic chessmen are abstract. Famous chessmen—such as the Lewis chessmen, the Charlemagne chess set, and sets used by the Founders of the United States—are featured.

Wolff, P. (2005). *The complete idiot's guide to chess* (3rd ed.). New York: Alpha Books. This book is a comprehensive introduction to the game of chess, similar to Eade (2005).

World Chess Boxing Organisation. (2009). *FAQ.* Retrieved from http:// wcbo.org/content/e686/index_en.html This Web page gives answers to frequently asked questions about chess boxing.

Photo Credits

All photos are by Alexey Root. The author photo was taken by Clarissa Root.

Appendix C

CHESS SCRIPTS

Appendix C has, in chronological order, three famous games and two chess problems. They may serve as the basis for living chess game scripts. The famous games accommodate up to 32–34 actors, that is, 32 living chessmen and the white and black players, who serve as narrators. If you have an actor surplus, the narrators do not have to be limited to two players. Instead, divide the narrator role into narrator one, narrator two, narrator three, and so forth.

I assume, however, that an actor shortage is more common than an actor surplus. Four strategies for overcoming a shortage, listed in the order they should be employed, are the following:

1. Chessmen that do not move and are not captured may be represented as set decorations.
2. Chessmen that are captured on their original squares may be represented as props.
3. Living chessmen captured early may take the place of set-decoration chessmen that are required to move or capture later in the game.
4. Narrators may double as their army's kings.

These strategies are further explained in the background description of each game and problem. For example, the Réti endgame requires just four actors but can accommodate up to seven (or more, by having multiple narrators).

Position after 2. f4

The King's Gambit

Figure C.1.

Position after 3. Bc4

The bishop attacks f7

Figure C.2.

The living chessmen move according to the algebraic notation in the script. For the one or two chessmen involved in each move or capture, the script may also incorporate *Activity Three* (musical themes for the moves of chessmen) and *Activity Four* (choreography to represent the chessmen's captures). The script may suggest appropriate facial expressions for other chessmen to make during the current chess move. For example, as the white queen is being captured the faces of the other white chessmen could express dismay.

For each game or problem, I provide the algebraic notation of the game or problem in boldface. Second, I present background material on the players or problem composer and tell how to accommodate an actor shortage. Third, I give annotations for several important moves. Annotations are for **intermediate** (not **beginning**) chess players and point out **tactics** such as **pins, forks, discovered check,** and **perpetual check.** I also note when one side is **material** ahead. I do not list variations that would be understood only by players with **ratings** higher than 1500 (USCF or **Fédération Internationale des Échecs [FIDE]**). I provide figures (chess diagrams) for annotated moves in the chess games and for the starting positions of the chess problems. I researched background and annotations in chess books (Chernev, 1955; Eade, 2005; Keres, 1973/1974; Shenk, 2006). Script writers, or those interested in advanced chess analysis, may further supplement with information from books or the Internet.

Immortal game, algebraic notation. **White: Anderssen; black: Kieseritzky. 1. e4 e5 2. f4 exf4 3. Bc4 Qh4+ 4. Kf1 b5 5. Bxb5 Nf6 6. Nf3 Qh6 7. d3 Nh5 8. Nh4 Qg5 9. Nf5 c6 10. g4 Nf6 11. Rg1 cxb5 12. h4 Qg6 13. h5 Qg5 14. Qf3 Ng8 15. Bxf4 Qf6 16. Nc3 Bc5 17. Nd5 Qxb2 18. Bd6 Bxg1 19. e5 Qxa1+ 20. Ke2 Na6 21. Nxg7+ Kd8 22. Qf6+ Nxf6 23. Be7# 1–0.**

Immortal game, background. White was Adolf Anderssen (1818–1879), a German and the world's strongest chess player at that

Position after 4. Kf1

Since white moved his K, he can't castle

Figure C.3.

Position after 4....b5

Bryan Countergambit

Figure C.4.

Position after 5. Bxb5

Material is equal

Figure C.5.

Position after 5....Nf6

Black attacks the e4-pawn

Figure C.6.

Position after 6. Nf3

White attacks the black queen

Figure C.7.

time. Black was Lionel Kieseritzky (1806–1853), a proficient coffee-house player who lived in France. According to David Shenk (2006):

Lionel Kieseritzky was an unpleasant sort of fellow—irritable, obtuse, and with a sharp tongue. Anderssen, by contrast, was a player's player. He had no apparent interests outside of chess, and was well liked by all who knew him—"honest and honourable to the core," remarked his frequent adversary Wilhelm Steinitz. (p. 135)

The game was played June 21, 1851, at the London chess café and men's club Simpson's Grand Divan Tavern. Both players were in London for an international tournament, but this game was an informal one. Later, Kieseritzky published it in his French chess journal. Upon reading the game in the journal, another master, Ernst Falkbeer, nicknamed it "The Immortal Game." Shenk (2006) praised Kieseritzky for publishing the game: "Broadcasting his own brutal loss was a testament to Kieseritzky's humility, his respect for Anderssen, and his devotion to the game" (p. 225). Every year since 1923, the town of Marostica, Italy, has replayed the Immortal game as a living chess game.

The Immortal game requires between 16 and 25 actors, though 32–34 could be used if available. The following 9 chessmen remain stationary, so they may be represented as set decorations: For white, the a- and c-pawns; for black, the a-, d-, f-, and h-pawns, the rooks on a8 and h8, and the bishop on c8. If these set decorations are in place, 23 actors may be cast as living chessmen and 2 more as the famous players. If fewer than 23–25 actors are available, props may also represent the chessmen captured on their original squares: For white, the b-pawn and the rook on a1; for black the g-pawn. With this further substitution of props for chessman, 20 chessmen roles remain. If fewer than 20 living chessmen are available, have the chessmen captured early, such as the white f-pawn and black b-pawn, take on roles of chessmen that move later, such as the white d-pawn and the black

Position after 7. d3

White protects e4 and attacks f4

Figure C.8.

Position after 7....Nh5

Threatens a fork on g3

Figure C.9.

Position after 8. Nh4

Stops Black's planned fork

Figure C.10.

Position after 8....Qg5

Queen forks two pieces

Figure C.11.

Position after 10. g4

Black does not want to play e.p.

Figure C.12.

c-pawn. Then just 18 actors portray chessmen. You might also have the actors portraying Anderssen and Kieseritzky serve double-duty as the white king and black king, respectively. Then only 16 actors are required to perform the Immortal game.

Immortal game, annotations. White: Anderssen; Black: Kieseritzky. **1. e4 e5 2. f4** White's second move characterizes the King's gambit, as shown in Figure C.1. White gambits the f-pawn to get control of the center. **2. . . . exf4 3. Bc4** White's third move is an attack on black's f7 pawn, a weak spot because it is defended only by the king, as shown in Figure C.2. White's f2 square is similarly weak. **3. . . . Qh4+ 4. Kf1** White could have blocked the check with g3, but that loses a pawn to fxg3. So he moved his king, as shown in Figure C.3. Now white will not be able to castle in this game. **4. . . . b5** Black's fourth move initiates the Bryan countergambit, as shown in Figure C.4. **5. Bxb5** White accepts the gambit pawn, so now material is equal. The resulting position is shown in Figure C.5. **5. . . . Nf6** Black's fifth move attacks the e-pawn, as shown in Figure C.6. **6. Nf3** With his sixth move, white's knight attacks the black queen (worth nine points). Thus black cannot afford to take the pawn (worth just one point) on this move. The position is shown in Figure C.7. **6. . . . Qh6 7. d3** White's seventh move protects the e4 pawn and opens a diagonal for the bishop on c1, as shown in Figure C.8. **7. . . . Nh5** Black's seventh move has the idea of 8. . . . Ng3+ forking the king on f1 and the rook on h1. White's h-pawn is pinned. That is, if 9. hxg3 Qxh1. With his next move, white defends against black's threat. The position after black's seventh move is shown in Figure C.9. **8. Nh4** Now if 8. . . . Ng3+, then the h-pawn (which is no longer pinned) would take it (9. hxg3). See Figure C.10. **8. . . . Qg5** Black's eighth move forks the white bishop on b5 and the white knight on h4 as shown in Figure C.11. **9. Nf5 c6 10. g4** This 10th-move double-jump by white's g-pawn allows the en passant capture 10. . . . fxg3. But en passant would be a bad idea, because

Position after 11. Rg1

White sacrifices the bishop

Figure C.13.

Position after 14. Qf3

Trying to trap the black queen

Figure C.14.

Position after 14....Ng8

Queen now has escape squares

Figure C.15.

Position after 15....Qf6

Queen attacks the b2-pawn

Figure C.16.

Position after 17. Nd5

Sacrificing material

Figure C.17.

of the reply 11. Bxg5. The position after white's 10th move is shown in Figure C.12 **10. . . . Nf6 11. Rg1** White sacrifices the bishop on b5, but defends the g-pawn and prepares a 12th-move attack on the black queen. The position is shown in Figure C.13. **11. . . . cxb5 12. h4 Qg6 13. h5 Qg5 14. Qf3** White's move 14, shown in Figure C.14, threatens 15. Bxf4, trapping the black queen. **14. . . . Ng8** The black knight retreats so that the queen has escape squares along the d8–h4 diagonal as shown in Figure C.15. **15. Bxf4 Qf6** Black's move 15 threatens to take on the white pawn on b2, as shown in Figure C.16. **16. Nc3 Bc5 17. Nd5** White's move 17 invites black to take a pawn and two rooks as shown in Figure C.17. **17. . . . Qxb2 18. Bd6 Bxg1 19. e5 Qxa1+ 20. Ke2 Na6** Black's move 20 defends against Nc7+, forking the black king and rook. But white has checkmate in mind. The position after 20. . . . Na6 is in Figure C.18. **21. Nxg7+ Kd8 22. Qf6+ Nxf6** If black instead chose 22. . . . Ne7, then white would have played 23. Qxe7#. The position after move 22 is in Figure C.19. **23. Be7# 1–0.**

Evergreen game, algebraic notation. **1. e4 e5 2. Nf3 Nc6 3. Bc4 Bc5 4. b4 Bxb4 5. c3 Ba5 6. d4 exd4 7. 0-0 d3 8. Qb3 Qf6 9. e5 Qg6 10. Re1 Nge7 11. Ba3 b5 12. Qxb5 Rb8 13. Qa4 Bb6 14. Nbd2 Bb7 15. Ne4 Qf5 16. Bxd3 Qh5 17. Nf6+ gxf6 18. exf6 Rg8 19. Rad1 Qxf3 20. Rxe7+ Nxe7 21. Qxd7+ Kxd7 22. Bf5+ Ke8 23. Bd7+ Kf8 24. Bxe7# 1–0**

Evergreen game, background. As in the Immortal game, Adolf Anderssen played white. Black was a German named Jean Dufresne (1820–1893). Dufresne was the author of chess books and a master. The game was played in 1852 in Berlin, Germany. The nickname "Evergreen" was taken from a comment by World Chess Champion Wilhelm Steinitz.

The Evergreen game requires between 19 and 24–26 actors, though 32–34 may be used if available. The following 8 chessmen

Position after 20....Na6

Defends c7

Figure C.18.

Position after 22....Nxf6

Black took white's queen

Figure C.19.

Position after 7....d3

The Evans Gambit

Figure C.20.

Position after 8. Qb3

White attacks f7

Figure C.21.

Position after 8....Qf6

Defends the f-pawn a second time

Figure C.22.

remain stationary, so they could be represented as set decorations: For white, the a-, f-, g-, and h-pawns; for black, the a-, c-, f-, and h-pawns. With these set decorations in place, 24 actors are needed as living chessmen and an additional 2 actors can portray Anderssen and Dufresne. If fewer than 24–26 actors are available, a prop may also represent the chessman (black pawn on d7) captured on its original square. If fewer than 23 chessmen-actors are available, have the chessmen that are captured early, such as the white b- and d-pawns, also portray the black b- and g-pawns. Then just 21 actors are chessmen. The Anderssen and Dufresne actors may serve double-duty as the white king and black king, respectively. Then only 19 actors are required to perform the Evergreen game.

Evergreen game, annotations. See *Reading and Writing Chess* in chapter 5 for an explanation of the first seven moves of this game. **1. e4 e5 2. Nf3 Nc6 3. Bc4 Bc5 4. b4 Bxb4 5. c3 Ba5 6. d4 exd4 7. 0-0 d3** Black's seventh move is not as good as either 7. . . . dxc3 (temporarily winning a pawn) or 7. . . . d6 (allowing the bishop on c8 to develop), according to Eade (2005, p. 281). The position after move 7 is shown in Figure C.20. **8. Qb3** Now there are two attackers (the white queen and bishop) and one defender (the black king) for the pawn on f7 as shown in Figure C.21. **8. . . . Qf6** defends the f7 pawn a second time as shown in Figure C.22. **9. e5 Qg6** Black did not choose 9. . . . Nxe5 because 10. Re1 d6 11. Qb5+ forks the king on e8 and the bishop on a5, winning the bishop (Eade, 2005, p. 281). Figure C.23 shows the position after the ninth move. **10. Re1 Nge7 11. Ba3 b5** Black sacrifices his b-pawn so that, when it is captured, black can develop his rook with **tempo.** But better was simply 11. . . . 0-0. The position after move 11 is in Figure C.24. **12. Qxb5 Rb8 13. Qa4 Bb6** If black had played 13. . . . 0-0 then 14. Bxe7 Nxe7 15. Qxa5 wins a piece. The position after move 13 is in Figure C.25. **14. Nbd2 Bb7 15. Ne4 Qf5 16. Bxd3** White threatens to move his knight to d6 or f6 with check and a **discovered attack** on

Position after 9....Qg6

Figure C.23.

Position after 11....b5

Black sacrifices a pawn

Figure C.24.

Position after 13....Bb6

Figure C.25.

Position after 16. Bxd3

White threatens a discovered attack

Figure C.26.

Position after 17. Nf6+

White N on f6 forks black K and Q

Figure C.27.

the black queen from the bishop on d3. So black moves his queen. The position after white's move 16 is in Figure C.26. **16. . . . Qh5 17. Nf6+** White's move 17 forks the black king and queen, but 17. Nd6+ would have been a simpler way to maintain white's advantage. The position after 17. Nf6+ is shown in Figure C.27. **17. . . . gxf6 18. exf6** After white's move 18, the black knight is now pinned to its king by the white rook on e1. Since the pin is absolute, it is illegal to move the black knight on e7 until the pin is broken. The position after white's move 18 is shown in Figure C.28. **18. . . . Rg8 19. Rad1 Qxf3** For move 19, black takes a piece and threatens Qxg2#. Better was 19. . . . Qh3, which threatens the same checkmate but also protects the d7 pawn. The position after move 19 is shown in Figure C.29. **20. Rxe7+ Nxe7 21. Qxd7+ Kxd7** If black had chosen 21. . . . Kf8, then 22. Qxe7#. Position after move 21 is shown in Figure C.30. **22. Bf5+** White's move 22 is a **double check** on black's king, from white's rook and bishop, as shown in Figure C.31. **22. . . . Ke8 23. Bd7+ Kf8 24. Bxe7# 1–0**

Opera game, algebraic notation. **1. e4 e5 2. Nf3 d6 3. d4 Bg4 4. dxe5 Bxf3 5. Qxf3 dxe5 6. Bc4 Nf6 7. Qb3 Qe7 8. Nc3 c6 9. Bg5 b5 10. Nxb5 cxb5 11. Bxb5+ Nbd7 12. 0-0-0 Rd8 13. Rxd7 Rxd7 14. Rd1 Qe6 15. Bxd7+ Nxd7 16. Qb8+ Nxb8 17. Rd8# 1–0.**

Opera game, background. White in the Opera game was Paul Morphy (1837–1884). Born in New Orleans, Louisiana, Morphy was a chess prodigy. He was also an excellent student, graduating college with high honors. He then studied law at the University of Louisiana (now Tulane University). Since he was too young to practice law when he received his LLB, he played chess. In 1858 he went to Europe to challenge the strongest players there and defeated Adolf Anderssen. The Opera game was an informal game played during a Paris opera performance. Historical accounts dispute which opera, but most cite *The Barber of Seville.* Two chess amateurs played black: the German noble Duke Karl of Brunswick

Position after 18. exf6

Figure C.28.

Position after 19....Qxf3

Black threatens checkmate

Figure C.29.

Position after 21....Kxd7

Figure C.30.

Position after 22. Bf5+

Double check

Figure C.31.

and the French aristocrat Count Isouard. The duke and the aristocrat consulted each other about which move to play. Eade (2005, p. 283) wrote, "Legend has it that the duke was roundly criticized in the next day's papers for playing a game of chess at the opera!"

The Opera game requires between 12 and 22 actors, though 32–35 may be used if available. The following 13 chessmen remain stationary, so they could be represented as set decorations: For white, the a-, b-, c-, f-, g-, and h-pawns; for black, the a-, f-, g-, and h-pawns, the king on e8, the bishop on f8, and the rook on h8. With these set decorations in place, 19 actors are needed as living chessmen and an additional 3 actors can portray Morphy, Brunswick, and Isouard. If fewer than 19–22 chessmen-actors are available, have the chessmen captured early, such as the white d-pawn, white kingside knight, black queenside bishop, and black e-pawn, take the place of props that move as chessmen later in the game. Then just 15 actors are chessmen. The Morphy, Brunswick, and Isouard actors may serve double-duty as the white king, black king, and black queen respectively. Then only 12 actors are required to perform the Opera game.

Opera game, annotations. **1. e4 e5 2. Nf3 d6** Black's second move makes this a Philidor **defense,** shown in Figure C.32. **3. d4 Bg4 4. dxe5 Bxf3** If black had chosen 4. . . . dxe5, then 5. Qxd8 Kxd8 6. Nxe5 wins a pawn. The position after the fourth move is in Figure C.33. **5. Qxf3 dxe5 6. Bc4** Now white threatens 7. Qxf7#. The position after 6. Bc4 is shown in Figure C.34. **6. . . . Nf6 7. Qb3** Now white threatens 8. Bxf7+ Kd7 9. Qe6#. The position after white's seventh move is in Figure C.35. **7. . . . Qe7 8. Nc3** White develops a knight instead of taking a pawn with 8. Qxb7, which would allow 8. . . . Qb4+, forcing a queen trade. The position after 8. Nc3 is shown in Figure C.36. **8. . . . c6 9. Bg5 b5 10. Nxb5** White's move 10 sacrifices a knight for two pawns. In compensation, white will have a lead in development. See Figure C.37. **10. . . . cxb5 11. Bxb5+ Nbd7 12. 0-0-0 Rd8** If black had chosen 12. . . . 0-0-0 then

Position after 2....d6

Philidor Defense

Figure C.32.

Position after 4....Bxf3

Figure C.33.

Position after 6. Bc4

With a threat of checkmate on f7

Figure C.34.

Position after 7. Qb3

Figure C.35.

Position after 8. Nc3

Figure C.36.

Position after 10. Nxb5

Sacrifice

Figure C.37.

13. Ba6+ Kc7 14. Qb7# (Chernev, 1955, p. 214). White's next two moves take advantage of the pinned knights on d7 and f6. See Figure C.38 for the position after move 12. **13. Rxd7 Rxd7 14. Rd1 Qe6** Black unpins his knight on f6 and offers a queen trade as shown in Figure C.39. **15. Bxd7+ Nxd7 16. Qb8+ Nxb8 17. Rd8# 1–0.**

Thirteen moves to checkmate, algebraic notation. Starting position, with white to play and win in 13 moves, is shown in Figure C.40: White: Kf8, Qa1, Rf7, Rg7. Black: Kh8, Qg1, Rh1, Bs on f1 and h6, Ng3, Ps on a3, e4, f2, f5, g6, h7. White to move. Solution: **1. Ke7 Bg5+ 2. Kd6 Bf4+ 3. Kc5 Be3+ 4. Kb4 Bd2+ 5. Kxa3 Bc1+ 6. Kb4 Bd2+ 7. Kc5 Be3+ 8. Kd6 Bf4+ 9. Ke7 Bg5+ 10. Kf8 Bh6 11. Qa8 Bxg7+ 12. Ke7+ Bf8+ 13. Qxf8# 1–0.**

Thirteen moves to checkmate, background. I found this problem on Stratakis (1994). Further research showed that the problem had originally been published by *American Chess Weekly* in 1909. Because we have little background information and not many annotations, the nonmoving pawns and pieces could repeatedly chant the annotation, "And the bishop had to check again." The following 13 chessmen remain stationary: For white, the rooks on g7 and f7; for black, the a-, e-, f2-, f5-, g-, and h-pawns, the king on h8, the queen on g1, the rook on h1, the bishop on f1, and the knight on g3. If you have an actor shortage, use set decorations for the nonmoving chessmen. Then three actors are needed as living chessmen. Of those three actors, the queen moves the least. Therefore, give a double role of narrator and white queen to an actor.

13 moves to checkmate, annotations. Starting position, with white to play and win in 13 moves, is shown in Figure C.40: White: Kf8, Qa1, Rf7, Rg7. Black: Kh8, Qg1, Rh1, Bs on f1 and h6, Ng3, Ps on a3, e4, f2, f5, g6, h7. White to move. Solution: **1. Ke7** with an ongoing threat of Rf8# on the next move, so black must keep checking. Black hopes to draw by perpetual check, but white can escape the checks and win. **1. . . . Bg5+ 2. Kd6 Bf4+ 3. Kc5 Be3+ 4. Kb5**

Position after 12....Rd8

Figure C.38.

Position after 14....Qe6

Figure C.39.

Starting positon for 13 moves problem

White to move

Figure C.40.

Starting positon for Réti problem

White to move

Figure C.41.

Bd2+ 5. Kxa3 Bc1+ 6. Kb4 Bd2+ 7. Kc5 Be3+ 8. Kd6 Bf4+ 9. Ke7 Bg5+ 10. Kf8 Bh6 Black pins the rook on g7 to the white king, thus preventing 11. Rg8#. **11. Qa8 Bxg7+ 12. Ke7+** White's move 12 is a discovered check. The white king's move uncovered the white queen's check. **12. . . . Bf8+ 13. Qxf8# 1–0.**

Réti endgame, algebraic notation. Starting position, with white to play and draw, is shown in Figure C.41: White: Kh8, pawn on c6. Black: Ka6, pawn on h5. Solution: **1. Kg7 h4 2. Kf6 Kb6 3. Ke5 h3 4. Kd6 h2 5. c7 Kb7 6. Kd7 h1(Q) 7. c8(Q)+ 1/2–1/2.**

Réti endgame, background. Richard Réti (1889–1929) was one of the top players in the world in the 1910s and 1920s. He lived in Prague, in what is now Slovakia. In 1925 he played 29 games blindfolded, winning 21 and drawing 6. He died of scarlet fever.

In 1921 Réti published this endgame problem. Staging it as a living chess game requires between four and seven actors. Typical would be to use just five actors: a white king, a white pawn, a black king, a black pawn, and Réti, to provide narration and annotations. If seven actors are available, two of them may be cast as the queens. If only four actors are available, the Réti actor may portray Réti and the white king.

Réti endgame, annotations. Starting position, with white to play and draw, is shown in Figure C.41: White: Kh8, pawn on c6. Black: Ka6, pawn on h5. Keres (1973/1974) wrote:

> Although White is to move, he appears hopelessly lost, for the black pawn is going to queen and White needs at least two tempi to stop it. His own pawn seemingly offers little hope as it can easily be stopped by the black king. (p. 13)

"Tempi" is the plural of *tempo*, which is a term defined in the glossary. Solution: **1. Kg7 h4 2. Kf6 Kb6** If black instead plays 2. . . . h3, then the game would continue 3. Ke7 h2 4. c7 and both pawns promote. **3. Ke5** White has the threat of 4. Kf4, catching the h-pawn. **3. . . . h3 4. Kd6 h2 5. c7 Kb7** Black could try 5. . . . h1(Q). Then white would continue with 6. c8(Q). **6. Kd7 h1(Q) 7. c8(Q)+ 1/2–1/2.**

Glossary

Algebraic notation is the most common notation system for writing chess moves. Each square has a name based on its file (a–h) and rank (1–8) coordinates. Short-form algebraic notation, used throughout this book, lists the name of the piece followed by the square it lands on. Long-form algebraic notation lists the starting square and the ending square for each move.

Annotations are comments on both good moves and mistakes. Depending on the annotator's goals and abilities, annotations give lessons to be learned from or the truth about a chess position.

Beginning scholastic chess players have 15 hours or less of chess experience. They are still learning the board, rules, and strategies of chess. In terms of USCF rating, they would be approximately 0–200.

Bishop (B) is a chess piece that moves diagonally along unoccupied squares. It can capture an enemy piece or pawn that is in its path. At the beginning of a game, each player has a light-squared bishop and a dark-squared bishop. A bishop is worth a little more than three pawns (three points), according to most sources.

Board is the arena for the chess game and is short for "chessboard." The board has 32 light squares and 32 dark squares in an alternating pattern. Squares are arranged in eight vertical columns, called files, and eight horizontal rows, called ranks. When the board is positioned correctly, the lower right corner is a white square. For chess teaching, acquire boards with algebraic notation marked on the borders of the board.

Captures occur when a pawn or piece moves to a square occupied by an enemy pawn or piece, except in the case of en passant. The capture removes the enemy piece or pawn from the board. You may not capture your own chessmen. The notation for a capture is a letter x; for example, exd5 means the e-pawn takes a chessman on d5 or Nxf6 means the knight takes a chessman on f6.

Castling (castle) is a move notated 0-0 (kingside castling, "castling short") or 0-0-0 (queenside castling, "castling long"). Castling can be done once per side, if the king and rook that want to castle with each other haven't moved previously and the king is not in check, crossing over a checked square, or ending on a checked square. Also, there can be no pieces between the king and rook during the castling move. To castle, the king moves two squares toward its rook, and the rook hops over the king and lands on the square horizontally adjacent to the king.

Center of the board includes the squares e4, d4, e5, and d5.

Check (+) is a direct attack on a king by an enemy piece or pawn. The king must get out of check by capturing the checking piece or pawn, blocking the check with one of his own men, or moving to a square that is not attacked.

Checkmate (+ + or # or mate) is when the king is in check and cannot escape from check. Being checkmated means that player has lost the chess game.

Chessmen are the "pieces and pawns considered as a group" (Pandolfini, 1995, p. 66).

Clocks are used to time chess games. A player's time runs when it is that player's move. At the completion of a move, the player punches a button to start the opponent's clock running. Some games use sudden death (SD) time controls. That is, a player must finish the whole game before the time elapses. Common SD time controls include G/5 (game in 5 minutes per player, called blitz or speed chess) and G/30 (game in 30 minutes per player, called action chess). G/30 is the fastest time control allowed for a game to be rated under the regular rating system by USCF; G/5–G/29 are rated under a separate quick chess rating system.

In contrast, some tournaments use traditional time controls such as 40/2, 20/1, 20/1: make 40 moves before your first two hours elapse, then make 20 moves per hour for the next two time controls. For both SD and traditional time controls, a loss on time (a flag fall) means a loss of the game, except when the side "winning on time" doesn't have sufficient material to deliver a checkmate (e.g., only has a K and a B or only has a K and an N; see *draw*).

Defense is "a move or series of moves designed to meet opposing threats and attacks, whether immediate or long range. In the openings, a defense is a system of play whose characteristic positions are determined largely by Black" (Pandolfini, 1995, p. 88).

Demonstration board (demo board) is a large, upright chess board that either hangs from a nail or map hook or is mounted on an easel. Its chessmen are held on magnetically or fit into slots. The demonstration board is used for showing chess moves to groups. Most chess retailers, including USCF, sell demonstration boards.

Descriptive notation is an older system of notation than algebraic notation. Descriptive notation is based on the names and squares that pieces occupy at the beginning of the game, for example, 1. Kt.–KB3 (or the Kt. to its K. B. third square) means knight to king's bishop's three. In short-form algebraic, that same move would be written 1. Nf3. In long-form algebraic, it would be 1. g1–f3.

Development involves moving pieces from their starting squares to squares that attack the center of the board or other important targets.

Diagonal is "a slanted row of same-colored squares. There are 26 different diagonals on the chessboard" (Pandolfini, 1995, p. 90).

Diagram is a two-dimensional representation of a chess position. Traditionally, the white chessmen start at the bottom of a chess diagram. To make diagrams by hand, abbreviate the chessmen's names (K, Q, R, B, N, and P) and circle the black chessmen. Or use a software program such as ChessBase Light, available from http://www.chessbase.com/download/index.asp, which includes fonts that give figurine representations of white and black pieces and pawns. Figure G.1 is a reproducible blank diagram.

Discovered attack is a movement of a piece or pawn uncovering an attack by an unmoved piece.

Discovered check is "the movement of a piece or pawn that results in a check by an unmoved piece" (Eade, 2005, p. 320).

Double check is a "discovered check in which the moved piece also gives check. Only the movement of the king can meet a double check" (Eade, 2005, p. 321).

Draws are scored as a half point for each player. As Eade (2005, p. 321) wrote, there are several ways for a draw to result: "(a) by agreement of both players, (b) by stalemate, (c) by the declaration and proof of one player that the same position has appeared three times (with the same player to move), (d) by the declaration and proof of one player that there have been 50 moves during which no piece [or pawn] has been taken and no pawns have been moved, although there are some exceptions to the 50 move rule." If a player runs out of time (see *clock*)—but the opponent doesn't have sufficient material to checkmate—a draw is declared. Finally, in some cases, tournament

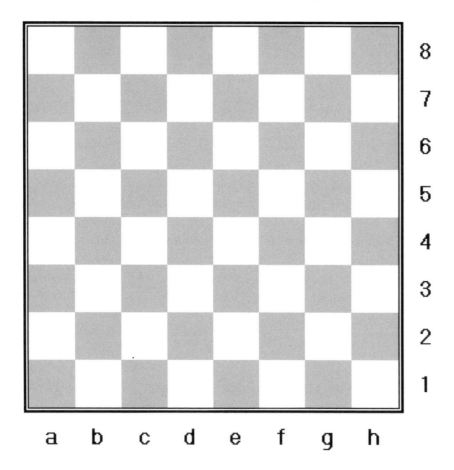

To make a diagram of a position, use the following abbreviations: P for white pawn, N for white knight, B for white bishop, R for white rook, Q for white queen, and K for white king. For example, a white rook on e4 is recorded by a letter R written on the e4 square.

Use the same abbreviations for black pieces and pawns, but circle them to show that a black piece or pawn is represented. For example, black rook on e6 is recorded by a ® (a circled letter R) on e6. Be sure to state which side is to move (white or black) at the bottom of this page.

Figure G.1.
Blank diagram.

directors may adjudicate games as draws, wins, or losses, usually when there is a time constraint to complete a club game or a team match.

En passant (e.p.) is French for "in passing" and is pronounced ahn pah-SAHNT. The en passant capture can be executed by pawns that are on a player's own fifth rank. On an algebraically-labeled board, the fifth rank for a black pawn is rank 4. When an enemy pawn does a double jump to the square adjacent to the fifth-rank pawn, then that pawn can capture the enemy pawn as if it had moved only one square. The en passant capture is optional. If chosen, en passant is played on the half-move immediately following the enemy pawn's double jump.

Endgame (ending) is the stage of the game that occurs after approximately 15 points in pieces (not pawns) have been exchanged for each side (Fine, 1941, p. 441). That is, if each side has traded off a queen and two minor pieces, then usually the position is classified as an endgame. Often the king becomes active in the endgame, attacking enemy pawns and supporting the promotion of his own pawns.

Fédération Internationale des Échecs (FIDE), Web site http://www.fide.com, is the world chess federation, with 161 countries (including the United States represented by USCF) as members. FIDE maintains a rating system and awards international titles such as Grandmaster (GM), International Master (IM), and FIDE Master (FM). FIDE also organizes world championships.

FIDE Master (FM) title can be earned by achieving a FIDE rating of over 2300 at some point in time.

Files are the vertical columns of squares on the board. There are eight files, labeled a, b, c, d, e, f, g, and h.

Forks are simultaneous attacks on two or more chess pawns or pieces.

Gambit is the offering of a pawn (or, more rarely, two pawns or a piece) in the opening for quick development, control of the center, or an attack on the king.

Grandmaster (GM) is an international title awarded by FIDE to players who perform above a predetermined level (2600 FIDE) at tournaments with other titled players. Usually it takes three such performances (three norms) to get the GM title.

Illegal move is one prohibited by the rules of chess. When noticed before the end of the game, it causes the position to be reset to just before the illegal move. At that point, a legal move must be played instead.

Intermediate scholastic chess players have 15 or more hours of chess instruction or playing experience. They already know the board, the rules, and some basic strategies of chess. They may already know how to read and write chess games. Their USCF rating or playing strength would be approximately 200–900.

International Master (IM) is a title awarded by FIDE to players who perform above a predetermined level (2451 FIDE) at tournaments with other titled players. Usually it takes three such performances (three norms) to get the IM title.

King (K) is able to move one square in any direction. The king captures the same way that it moves. When the king is checkmated or stalemated, the game is over. See also *castling*.

Kingside is the half of the board that includes the e-, f-, g-, and h-files.

Knight (N) is the piece that looks like a horse. Like a horse, it can jump over pieces and pawns. The knight's move is in the shape of a capital L. Or the knight's move can be described as two squares horizontally followed by one square vertically, or two squares vertically followed by one square horizontally. It captures an enemy chessman by landing on the square of that chessman. The knight is generally said to be worth three pawns (three points).

Ladder games are played at the pace of one game against one opponent per meeting session. Winning a game may move a player onto the ladder or higher up on the ladder.

Losses can occur because of checkmate, a loss on time (see *clock*), or because of resigning. A loss is scored as a zero.

Masters possess a USCF rating between 2200 and 2400. Those with ratings above 2400 are senior masters or are referred to by their FIDE titles.

Material refers to captured chessmen. If you have captured more points than your opponent, then you are material ahead.

Middlegame is the phase between the opening and the endgame. While specific openings and endings may be memorized, middlegames feature long-term strategies and calculations of tactics.

Moves in chess refer to either the move made for one side (i.e., half of a move pair) or the combined white and black move pair. Thus when a chess problem reads, "White to move," it is white's turn. But when the problem states, "White checkmates in three moves," that means three white moves (with the required black moves also played), in other words, a white move and black move, a second white move and black move, and a third white move completing the mate.

Opening refers to the first 10 or so moves of a chess game, during which time players develop most or all of their pieces. The opening is followed by the middlegame, which is followed by the endgame.

Pawns (P) are the smallest units on the chessboard. They move forward but capture diagonally. A pawn may move one or two squares on its initial move. When it reaches its eighth rank, it is promoted. See also *promoting* and *en passant*. A pawn is worth one point.

Perpetual check is when one side may check the other side's king continually and the checked side is unable to stop the checks. The game is a draw either by agreement or as a case of the threefold repetition of position rule. See also *draw*.

Pieces are not pawns but are kings, queens, rooks, bishops, and knights.

Pins immobilize lower-value pawns or pieces, because those chessmen must shield a higher-value piece from an enemy queen, rook, or bishop. The lower-value pawn or piece is pinned if when it moves the higher-value piece could be captured by the enemy. For example, a white bishop could pin a black knight to a black queen. If the knight moved off the bishop's diagonal, the white bishop could take the black queen. The previous example is a relative pin, because the knight could legally move. An absolute pin occurs when the higher-value piece is the king. In that case the pinned piece cannot legally move, as moving would expose the king to check.

Points are a guide for the fair exchange of pieces. That is, just as you wouldn't want to trade nine dollars for three dollars, you would likewise usually refuse to trade a Q (nine points) for an N (three points). The other point values are P (one point), B (three points), and R (five points). The king does not have points, since he cannot be traded, but his value is between three and four points. Points can also refer to a player's score in a tournament, for example, "She has one point" means that she either won one game or drew two games. Points can also refer to chess rating, as in "Alexey Root's January 2010 USCF rating is 2000, which is more than 250 points below her peak rating of 2262."

Position is the arrangement of the pieces and pawns on the board.

Problem is a chess position, usually represented on a diagram, for which there is a specific solution. For example, a problem might state, "White to move and mate in three." The person studying the problem would either set up the diagrammed position on a chess board to figure out the three moves or solve the problem mentally.

Promoting or Promotion is when a pawn reaches its eighth rank and is converted to an N, B, R, or Q. Players usually queen a pawn, as a queen is the piece worth the most points. Promoting to any piece except the queen is called underpromoting or underpromotion.

Queen is worth about nine pawns (nine points), according to most sources. On any given move, she can choose to move like a rook or like a bishop.

Queenside is the half of the board that includes the d-, c-, b-, and a-files.

Ranks are the horizontal rows of squares on a board. There are eight ranks, labeled 1, 2, 3, 4, 5, 6, 7, and 8 in algebraic notation.

Rating is a number assigned to a player based on his or her performance against other rated players. USCF ratings range from the low 100s to around 2800. More about ratings is at http://main.uschess.org/content/blogsection/14/195/.

Rook (R) is a chess piece that moves horizontally and vertically. It may move on squares that are not blocked by chessmen of its own color. It can capture an enemy piece or pawn that is in its path. The rook is usually said to be worth five pawns (five points). See also *castling*.

Sacrifices "deliberately give up material to achieve an advantage" such as a checkmating attack against the enemy king (Eade, 2005, p. 335).

Set of chessmen is the combined collection of 16 pawns, 4 rooks, 4 knights, 4 bishops, 2 queens, and 2 kings. Half the set are black pieces and pawns; half are white.

Simul (simultaneous exhibition) is when a single strong chess player plays several people all at the same time. "Numerous boards are set up, in a circle or rectangle, and the single player stands inside this area, moving from board to board, usually playing a single move at a time" (Eade, 2005, p. 336).

Stalemate is when a king is not in check but there are no legal moves for his side. It is scored as a draw.

Staunton chess sets are required at FIDE tournaments. Created by Nathaniel Cook in 1835, the design is named after the great English player Howard Staunton (Eade, 2005, p. 337).

Tactics are moves that force short-term sequences to win material or another advantage. Some common tactics are pins and forks.

Tempo is Italian for "time." To gain a tempo is to gain a move. For example, if your move forces your opponent to retreat disadvantageously, you have gained a tempo because it is now your turn again. The plural of "tempo" is *tempi*.

Touch move rule states that if players touch a particular pawn or piece, then they have to move it. If they touch an opponent's pawn or piece, then they must capture it. Once they remove their hand from a chessman, the move is completed and cannot be changed. If a legal move is impossible with the touched pawn or piece, another move must be selected. If a chessman simply needs to be straightened, say, "I adjust" (or the French term *J'adoube*), and then replace the pawn or piece on its square without penalty.

Tournaments are chess contests for more than two players.

Trades exchange your pawns or pieces for your opponent's.

United States Chess Federation (USCF) has a main Web site (http://www.uschess.org) and a sales Web site (http://www.uscfsales.com/). The USCF is the official governing body for chess in the United States. It also runs the USCF rating system, which ranks member players. USCF produces two magazines: *Chess Life*'s instructional articles are at the intermediate level and higher; *Chess Life for Kids* provides intermediate-level articles for children 12 and under.

Variations are alternatives to the moves that were actually played in the game under analysis. Variations are also "any sequence of moves united by a logical, purposeful idea, either played in a game or proposed by an analyst. Also a specific opening line, such as the Dragon Variation of the Sicilian Defense" (Pandolfini, 1995, p. 261).

Wins in chess occur when one player checkmates the other player or when that player's opponent resigns or loses on time (see *clock*). A win is scored as one point for the winning player on the tournament wall chart.

Index

About the Author

Dr. ALEXEY W. ROOT was the 1989 U.S. Women's Chess Champion and is the author of four previous books on chess in education: *Children and Chess: A Guide for Educators* (2006); *Science, Math, Checkmate: 32 Chess Activities for Inquiry and Problem Solving* (2008); *Read, Write, Checkmate: Enrich Literacy with Chess Activities* (2009); and *People, Places, Checkmates: Teaching Social Studies with Chess* (2010).

Alexey Root has a PhD in education from UCLA. She is a senior lecturer in the School of Interdisciplinary Studies at The University of Texas at Dallas (UTD). From 1999 to 2003 she served as the associate director of the UTD Chess Program, one of the best college chess teams in the United States. Root currently teaches UTD's Chess in Education Certificate online courses. She lives in Denton, Texas, with her husband, Doug; children, Clarissa and William; and rabbit, Abba.

Contact Dr. Root at alexey.root@gmail.com.